OVERCOMING
ADVERSITY

OVERCOMING ADVERSITY

RESETTING GOALS

NELSON J FOWLKES

ARPress
ILLUMINATING IDEAS
EMPOWERING VOICES

ARPress
45 Dan Road Suite 5
Canton MA 02021

Hotline: 1(888) 821-0229
Fax: 1(508) 545-7580

Ordering Information:

Quantity sales. Special discounts are available on quantity purchases by corporations, associations, and others. For details, contact the publisher at the address above.

Printed in the United States of America.

ISBN-13:   Softcover   979-8-89330-060-4
               eBook   979-8-89330-061-1

Library of Congress Control Number: 2024901197

TABLE OF CONTENTS

Introduction   vii

Chapter 1: My Arrival   1

Chapter 2: Life on the Farm   3

Chapter 3: Life with Biological Family   5

Chapter 4: Educational Pursuits   9

Chapter 5: My Life Partner   19

Chapter 6: Military Services Career   21

Chapter 7: Military Assignment   25

Chapter 8: Military Service Termination   41

Chapter 9: Promotion Board Lawsuit   43

Chapter 10: Health Care Career   45

Chapter 11: Educational Benifits   57

Chapter 12: Spiritual Development   59

Chapter 13: Adventurous Lifestyle   63

Chapter 14: Cycling My Passion   67

Chapter 15: Leisure Travel Business   75

Chapter 16: Exploring Family Connections   79

Chapter 17: Meaningful Retirement Life   83

Chapter 18: Return to Northern California   87

Closing   89

Dedication   91

Acknowledgments   93

About the author   95

INTRODUCTION

An adversity may be more than a mere misfortune or situation that work against you. It may be a series of barriers and obstacles that keep you from achieving your goals and dreams. Adversity comes in many forms: social injustice, discrimination, emotional distress, lack of financial resources or personal tragedy.

As humans, we face challenges and obstacles that adversely affect our goals and dreams. These unwelcome experiences can lead to pain, self-pity, hopelessness, and depression. Nevertheless, we should not let our misfortunes and troubles define us.

On my life journey, I experienced a series of setbacks, roadblocks, misfortunes, and obstacles that made it difficult and challenging to reach my goals and dreams. I had a fractured early childhood, and my teenage years were spent with different family members.

My family was poor, with very few resources. My parents were divorced and no one in my family had a college education. I moved frequently during my early years. As a toddler, I lived with my biological family in Tennessee, early childhood (birth -4) with surrogate parents in Georgia. After high school graduation I lived with an uncle in Cleveland, Ohio.

I didn't have financial resources or a well-thought-out action plan how to pursue my goals. However, I pressed forward with trust and faith in God, courage, self-confident and perseverance that my vision of getting an education and creating a better life for myself would be realized.

CHAPTER 1
My Arrival

In Chattanooga, Tennessee on December 26, 1934, Edward Bernard Fowlkes, and Dorothy Nelson Fowlkes celebrated the arrival of their new son whom they named Nelson—I was the fourth child of their relationship. My siblings included an older brother, Edward Bernard Jr., and two sisters, Doris Katrina, and Odessa Lee.

At the time of my birth, my parents experienced marital challenges regarding the uncertainty of who my father really was. As the conflict escalated and ten- sions grew, Uncle Charles and Aunt Amanda, close confidants of my parents, offered a solution to avoid divorce and sustain their marriage—I was sent to live with my cousin Odessa Gardner in Curryville, Georgia.

CHAPTER 2
Life on the Farm

My surrogate parents for the next six years were Reverend R.G. Gardner, a minister and farmer, and his wife, Odessa Gardner, a schoolteacher, and housewife. The Gardeners lived in a large white house on a hill overlooking a rural dirt road that ran from Calhoun to Rome. Curryville was an unincorporated community in Gordon County, somewhere between the cities of Calhoun and Dalton. (Roland Hayes, an acclaimed American lyric tenor, and composer also lived in Curryville for many years, and I had the privilege of meeting him.)

At the back and to one side of the house was a large tract of land for raising animals and growing fruits and vegetables. I was assigned various chores around the house and on the farm and gained valuable agriculture experience planting and harvesting fruits and vegetables, raising chickens, curing beef, catching rabbits and possums. Meat was preserved in the smokehouse until the next summer because refrigeration was limited. Cousin Odessa canned fruits, and vegetables and made fruit jams and jellies for the winter season. Each Saturday, we drove to Calhoun to shop and sell fruits and vegetables.

I attended school in a one-room schoolhouse where Cousin Odessa taught. I saw other children at school and at church, but I didn't know where they lived; in the country, families live great distances from each other. Apparently, I advanced from one grade level to the next, but I didn't know how the process worked.

The value system I gained from the Gardner's was based on Christian principles. When I was about ten years old, the Gardner's expressed interest in adopting me because they were childless. But my mother said, "No," and I was returned to my parents' home on the west side near downtown Chattanooga.

CHAPTER 3
Life with Biological Family

In 1944, I returned to Chattanooga to live with my biological family and became aware of two sisters, Doris, and Odessa, and a brother Edward Jr., who was seventeen years old. During World War II, my brother and father served in the navy and army respectively and discharged in 1945.

My brother participated in nuclear testing in the South Pacific and experienced some adverse effect from the testing. When he returned home from military service, he became an excessive drinker and failed to keep a steady job. Even though he would read every page in the daily newspaper, his limited formal education restricted him to minimum wage jobs as a janitor or dishwasher at restaurants. He lived most of his adult life at home until he married a woman who had seven children.

After my father's discharge from military service, he worked at a local foundry but did not maintain steady employment. Martial conflict developed because of frequent unemployment and eventually resulted in divorce. During my teenage years, I didn't have much opportunity to spend time with my father and get to know him. After the divorce, my father moved to Huntsville, Alabama, where he got work as a custodian at a local public school and later remarried. Several years after their divorce, my mother married a retired military veteran.

The living conditions in Chattanooga were vastly different from Curryville. Our house on Grove Place was perched on a hilly area a short walk from the city center. It was a shot gun house, a narrow rectangular house no more than twelve-feet wide, in a neighborhood of shot gun houses. If I stood in the front yard, I could look right through the house from front to back. We didn't have an indoor bathroom; bathing took place in a tin tub. Ice was purchased to put in the ice box to keep food cool. A wood-burning stove was used for cooking. At night, before bedtime, we'd sit around an open fireplace to stay warm; there was no heat in the bedroom. When I arose in the morning, the house was always cold, and I had to start a fire in the kitchen stove so breakfast could be prepared. We lived there for two years before moving to Blackford Street to live with my grandmother in East Chattanooga.

In Curryville, I wasn't aware of racism or discrimination. When I went to Chattanooga, however, I was much older and more observant. I felt I was being treated like someone inferior, like a non-human; racism and discrimination seemed normal for black Americans. Our schools, drinking fountains, parks and recreational facility activities were separate and unequal. Any food I purchased at a restaurant had to be ordered as takeout and picked up at the restaurant's back door or side window. I learned to adjust and cope with the situation.

Family has always been important to me. Throughout my life, different people in my family have influenced me, making a difference in my value system, my thinking, and the person I became. When I returned to Chattanooga, my mother became the central figure in my life, along with my extended family: my paternal grandmother, Sally Fowlkes; Uncle Percy, my father's brother; Aunt Mary; and my cousin Carrie Jefferson. My extended family lived a short walking distance from our house. I would visit them frequently at lunch or dinner, always hopeful I would be asked to share their meal. There was no central heat in their house, but each room had its own fireplace. I was always grateful to sit in front of the fireplace and talk with Grandmother Fowlkes.

After we moved to Blackford Street to live with my maternal grandmother, Della McDermott, our living conditions improved. I shared a bedroom with my brother, and my brother helped me avoid punishment from my mother when I was out late by letting me climb through our bedroom window. Over the years, our relationship became stronger. I appreciated him and enjoyed the stories about his military experiences that he shared with me.

As a single parent, my mother struggled to pay the monthly expenses. All of us children were required to find jobs to help with the expenses. At the age of thirteen, I began working to help with household expenses and small items for myself. I mowed lawns and picked fruit, such as blackberries, strawberries, and watermelons. My mother was a smart woman but, without a formal education, she had to work as a housemaid and would get home late in the evening. At one job, my mother worked as the housemaid while I mowed the lawn. At lunchtime, the homeowner (a white lady) made a distinction between us: my mother was allowed to eat lunch inside the house while I had to eat lunch on the back steps. Therefore, we even experienced discrimination as family members working together.

After this, I got a job at the Third Street Pharmacy as a helper and was eventually promoted to short order cook and soda fountain clerk. Third Street Pharmacy was a popular social gathering place for teens and adults. Inside the pharmacy was a seating area and coin-operated jukebox that played the latest tunes. The owner of the pharmacy was an African American. He had lost his license to sell prescription medications and was only authorized to sell over-the- counter medications. He also sold snacks, sandwiches, candy, and ice cream. It became apparent that he didn't trust his employees because he had a one-way mirror installed allowing him to monitor activities from his office, especially those operating the cash register.

My maternal grandmother, Della, lived across the street from the pharmacy and the Third Street Baptist Church next door to it. In 1946, her husband passed away and his children forced her to move. Before her marriage, Della had a house on Blackford Street in East Chattanooga where her son, my Uncle Nelson, and his wife, my Aunt Ethel, were living. When my grandmother was forced to move, her health was declining, and she chose my mother to be her caregiver. So, Uncle Nelson and Aunt Ethel had to move, and this created tension and resentment between my mother and her brother.

Uncle Nelson and Aunt Ethel moved to Cleveland where she had relatives, and, shortly afterwards, started their family, which came to include three children: Errol, Dwight, and Patricia. Uncle Nelson worked as a porter on the railroad and traveled frequently; he was well known within the passenger train industry. Despite the poor feeling between Uncle Nelson and my mother, I was always welcome and treated extremely well whenever I visited. When I was seventeen years old, I moved to Cleveland and visited them frequently, sometimes riding the bus, sometimes walking the eight-mile distance to their home.

As a teenager, one of my dreams was to own a bicycle. My family never had the financial means to make my dream a reality. When I was a student in middle school, I borrowed a school friend's bicycle to ride around in the neighborhood. but did not know how to adequately stop the bicycle. I eventually rode down the steep Orchard Knob hill that ended at the Third Street intersection. The east–west streetcar line ran along Third Street. I remember starting down the hill and waking up in the hospital. I was told that I crashed into a streetcar at the intersection. It was a miracle and blessing from God that I didn't suffer any broken limbs, brain injury or death. Surely, God had a fence of protection around me for which I am most grateful.

I believe we are, in part, a product of our experiences and environment. My childhood environment and experiences were quite different from my siblings'. These differences gave me a feeling of detachment and loosely connected to my nuclear family. I was only around my siblings for a short period of time. After I moved to Cleveland at age seventeen, I never returned to Chattanooga to live, only to visit. I had a strong desire to pursue a college education and obtain knowledge, skills, habits, and values to elevate myself above my poverty and improve my economic potential. It was my belief that a college education would be my pathway to a better life.

CHAPTER 4
Educational Pursuits

At the age of ten, I returned to Chattanooga and found school was quite different from the one-room schoolhouse where Cousin Odessa taught. In Chattanooga, I was enrolled in the public school system as a fifth-grade student at the Main Street Elementary School. When my family moved to Blackford Street, I attended Orchard Knob Junior High School for grades six to nine. At Orchard Knob, I had difficulty with technical and graphic images such as drawing and woodshop. My challenge was visualizing the third dimension of an image. Ninth grade algebra was also challenging for me. I repeated algebra at Howard High School, a black high school centrally located downtown, which was convenient to get to by walking or public transportation.

At one point in high school my grades began to decline. An English teacher offered me advice and encouragement. When he didn't see any improvement, he made a home visit to meet with my mother to express his interest and concern. This demonstration of interest in me became the spark and motivation that was needed for me to show improvement and make a commitment to always do my best in all things. This teacher's intervention was a blessing from God. I showed my grateful appreciation to the teacher by sending greeting cards and personally visiting him whenever I was in Chattanooga.

I believe God placed people in my life at different times for a specific purpose. During my high school years, I held a part time job as a bicycle delivery clerk at the largest and most prominent pharmacy in Chattanooga. My job was to deliver prescription and medical supplies to customers home or business loca- tion. Even though several delivery clerks were employed, the co-owner took a special interest in me. He encouraged me and talked about the attributes of high values, honesty, trustworthiness, and hard work as being major ingredients for achieving success in life. He suggested, if possible, I should leave Chattanooga after high school graduation, because there were limited job opportunities for African American males with only a high school diploma.

I had a strong desire to pursue a college education but no knowledge of the college admission process or even how to search for a college. Through an acquaintance of my youngest sister, I learned of three institutions of higher learning: Western Reserve University in Cleveland, Ohio; Central State University in Wilberforce, Ohio; and Tennessee State University in Nashville, Tennessee. I was told by some of my high school friends that Tennessee State was a party school and I observed that many students from Chattanooga who'd enrolled there returned home within the first year.

After graduating from high school, I went to Cleveland to live with Uncle Charles and Aunt Amanda. They lived on 120th Street approximately four blocks from Kinsman Road, the major east–west bus route. My goal was to achieve resident status in Ohio so I could qualify for lower fees at a state-supported university. First, I attempted to enroll at Western Reserve. I was administered a battery of test to determine my level of preparation for college work but unhappily failed the tests. At this point in my life, I was unsophisticated about a lot of things; only later did I realize that I didn't possess the academic strength to be successful at a major white university. It only now enters my thinking that black students were not welcome.

I felt frustrated and disappointed that my education at a black inner-city high school wasn't adequate preparation to compete with predominantly white students from better schools in more affluent neighborhoods. This was my first encounter with institutional racism and discrimination in the education system and the consequences of living in a society that promoted separate but not equal, despite the promises of our declaration of independence: "all men are created equal and endowed by their Creator with certain unalienable Rights: Life, Liberty and the pursuit of Happiness."

If I had been admitted, I had no idea of how my college expenses would be paid. Nevertheless, I continued to press forward; I didn't allow the setback to dampen my spirit or my goal of getting a college education. I looked for other opportunities to reset my path and direction, and enrolled at John Carroll University, a Catholic institution, where I took enrichment classes.

In 1952, I got a job at the Halle Brothers department store in downtown Cleveland and began saving up to attend Central State University, a predominantly black university in Wilberforce, Ohio. First, I worked in the barber shop with an older African American man who had seniority and a well-established customer base, which meant I got few customers. Later, I transferred to the laundry department and was responsible for cleaning display fabrics and table coverings. After accumulating some savings, I prepaid my first semester tuition at Central State.

A few weeks before traveling to Central State, I was in downtown Cleveland when an excited man approached me. He said he'd just won the sweepstakes and would share the money with me. As a show of good faith, he asked me to place several hundred dollars in a white envelope and put it in a specific mailbox on the street. I did as he asked, but then after we'd parted, I realized I didn't know the man's name or how he could be contacted. As the "light went on," I rushed back to the mailbox to try to get back the envelope, but it was impossible. I was the victim of a pigeon drop scam. Apparently, some guy had been monitoring my movements in the vicinity where I worked. This event, although painful, taught me a lifelong lesson: there is no free lunch and be careful of greed. The other thing I learned was to always be alert about your surroundings.

UNDERGRADUATE TRAINING

In September 1953, I began my freshman year at Central State University. As part of the admission process, I took a battery of standardized tests to determine my academic potential and aptitude. Surprisingly, I scored high in sales even though I'd previously had an unsuccessful sales experience. As a Fuller Brush salesman, I went door to door and customers placed their orders with me, promising to pay on delivery of the merchandise. To increase my total sales and commission, I paid for the merchandise beforehand. When, several customers refused to accept their order, I was left with unneeded inventory and lost compensation.

After enrolling at Central State, I received financial assistance in the form of work as a kitchen helper in the student cafeteria; later I was promoted to cashier. At the end of the first semester, I was pleasantly surprised to find my academic performance (a 3.25 grade point average) qualified me for the dean's list and I was subsequently awarded an academic scholarship. The rest of my college expenses were paid through a variety of sources including Uncle Booker
T. Fowlkes, who lived in Columbus, Georgia; scholarships from private organizations; a stipend from the Reserve Officers' Training Corps, or ROTC; and a part-time job at spring break and summer vacations with vendors that had maintenance and restoration projects at the university.

Central State was owned and operated by the African Methodist Episcopal Church. The university was established in 1887 at Wilberforce University which offered a four-year program and a two-year program to provide teacher training and industrial training. In 1941, Central State gained a four-year curriculum and in 1951, independent status. By 1965, full university status was achieved. Central State and Wilberforce University are located on opposite sides of a ravine. Today, Wilberforce is located on the opposite side of the highway. Central State continues to be primarily an African American university and is now considered a historically black university.

Central State offered a college-based program for training commissioned officers for the United States Armed Forces through ROTC. All male students were required to take basic training for two years. Admission to advanced training was by application, academic performance, and recommendation from a reserve training instructor—my application for the advanced training program was accepted. This was a huge blessing because the benefits for participation in the advanced program included a monthly stipend in the third and fourth years, six weeks of active-duty training at an active military base at the end of the second academic year, an opportunity to receive a reserve officer commis- sion as second lieutenant in the U.S. Army Reserve, and an obligation to serve two years of active military service after graduation. The stipend helped pay my college expenses.

In 1956, at the end of my third year in advanced officer training, I went with other eligible Central State students to Fort Bragg, North Carolina, an airborne training facility, for six weeks of mandatory basic military training. When we got there, Fort Bragg base officials informed the African American trainees that the nearest town to the base, Fayetteville, was off limits because the community openly discriminated against black Americans—and yet these same people, these locals, and public officials, wanted African Americans to go to foreign lands to defend Americans and keep our homeland safe. This hypoc- risy was just one more example of institutional racism.

One weekend, I went by automobile with several friends to Myrtle Beach in South Carolina (a round trip of 235 miles) for a fun day at the beach. When we finally arrived, we found a beautiful beach that happened to be for white people only. We were directed to the beach for Negroes; of course, it was unsuitable, and we did not stay. We were future military officers who were expected to die for our country, yet we were treated as inferiors. It clearly demonstrated to us that there was a so-called privileged class that didn't want to accept anyone unless they were white. But I knew God created all people and did not designate a superior race, although he did have his chosen people. When I lived in Chattanooga, the most prominent professional African Americans were physicians, dentists, teachers, business owners and lawyers. My mother wanted me was to pursue medical training and become a physi- cian. So, at Central State, I enrolled in pre-medicine and that discipline was my major emphasis until my senior year. At the end of my third year, I began to have doubts about how my medical school expenses would be paid. Rather than maintaining my faith and trust in God who had guided me through three years at Central State, I decide to change my direction, and this created complications by putting me on a technical track which changed my future direction and career.

GRADUATE TRAINING AT IOWA STATE

I was offered a graduate teaching assistantship to pursue graduate training in chemistry at three major universities, including Northwestern University in Evanston, Illinois; University of Montana in Missoula, Montana; and Iowa State University in Ames, Iowa. The graduate teaching assistantship was a work study program that helped pay my education expenses and gave me university-level teaching experience. On the recommendation of a chemistry professor at Central State, I accepted the teaching assistantship at Iowa State, where I served as the laboratory instructor for freshman engineering and home economic students who were required to take a basic chemistry class.

The winter season in Ames, Iowa, was extremely cold with the wind chill showing temperatures below zero. My roommate in the dormitory was a white graduate student from Rochester, New York, who was comfortable with the cold weather. He was not only unfriendly; he wanted to keep the room cold and the window open. I tried to keep the heat on and maintain a nice, warm, comfortable temperature for myself. We played yoyo through the winter, opening, and closing the window. When I was in the room alone, I'd manage to make the room nice and warm; when my roommate was alone in the room, he kept the room cold with the window open. The unpleasant atmosphere was a challenge between us.

I began to wonder if the cold and windy weather was perhaps a reflection of the treatment I would get from others as well. To pursue graduate training, I needed to be accepted into a chemistry professor's study group. The chosen professor would serve as my adviser and mentor to guide my course work and supervise my research project. But no chemistry professor was willing to accept me into their study group. I felt disappointed, frustrated, rejected and angry because this was the same university that granted me an assistantship. I didn't understand how the academic staff could be so mean spirited and hypocritical.

Fortunately, there was a biochemistry professor who had an African American graduate student in his group. Even though biochemistry wasn't my major, the professor displayed courage, sensitivity, and compassion by accepting me into his study group. Despite the obvious racism and discrimination at an institution of higher learning no less, I maintained my faith and hope.

But then a more devastating situation surfaced. I was informed by the admissions office that I'd failed to pass a battery of tests covering the major course material taught at Central State University. My major subjects at Central State included analytical chemistry, organic chemistry, physical chemistry, algebra, trigonometry, analytic geometry, and calculus. Consequently, I would not be enrolled in the advanced degree program at Iowa State. After failing to pass admissions test a second time, I felt depressed and began to doubt my abilities and potential.

So, I asked myself two questions: Did I fail to pass the test because I had attended a predominantly black educational institution that wasn't equal to mainstream institutions of higher learning? Or could it be that in 1957 few black students were accepted at white institutions because of discrimination? My situation reinforced the disadvantages of living in a segregated society that promotes separate but not equal.

Even though I experienced disappointments and setbacks at Iowa State, I remained optimistic and viewed life through the lens of opportunity and achievement, not despair and defeat. I continued to believe and trust in God and exercise the faith to pursue a different strategy for obtaining a graduate degree. At the end of the year at Iowa State, I went to Fort Sam Houston, Texas, to begin active military service.

BIOCHEMISTRY GRADUATE TRAINING AT UNIVERSITY OF TENNESSEE

I went to Vietnam in July 1966 and returned to the United States in 1967; the army approved my request for graduate training to begin in September 1968. I chose the University of Tennessee for a two-year biochemistry training. This choice had special significance for me. First, I was born in Tennessee and in 1952 graduated from a Tennessee high school. Second, in earlier years, admission would have been a challenge because of discrimination.

There were three African American students in the program, and we formed a study group built on bonds of trust and fellowship, with the goal of maximizing our individual and collective learning success. The pace of graduate training was strenuous, steady, and comprehensive. The study group was instrumental in helping me gain a better understanding and mastery of the material. I pursued my research project on the testosterone binding-globulin in the rabbit at the Veterans Affairs Medical Laboratory.

One biochemistry professor who had observed my character and academic performance invited me to stay and pursue a doctorate degree under his leadership. I was amazed, deeply honored, and appreciative of his interest and confidence in me. The professor offered to send a letter of support to the army. I was interested and honored but somewhat fearful that the extension would be viewed as selfish, that I would be seen as not being grateful and appreciative of what the army had already done for me. Therefore, I did not request the extension. I later found out that the army officer who approved graduate school extensions was a friend and fellow graduate of the Medical Service Corps Advanced Course. Many times, in life, we don't know the source from whence our blessings may come.

By this time, I was married with children, and finding a house in an excellent Memphis neighborhood with good quality schools was a priority and a challenge. I located a three-bedroom house for lease in East Memphis in a predominantly white community. The house was owned by a white family from California, and they also lived in the neighborhood. My wife and I met with the husband and his wife and informed them I was a major on active military duty and would be a graduate student for two years at the University of Tennessee. The neighborhood was made up of modest homes with well-maintained yards. My family became a test case as the first African American family to live in the neighborhood.

Some of the neighbors acted on their prejudices and didn't want the owners to lease the house to us. In fact, some met with the owners and offered to buy the house. At that point, the only thing the neighbors knew about us was our skin color. While the rejection was a demoralizing experience, the owners maintained their integrity and moral courage and leased the house to us. The neighbors reluctantly accepted us once they became aware that I was an active-duty military officer who would be going to graduate school at the university, my wife was a schoolteacher and we had three children.

In California, our children had attended public schools in San Rafael and San Francisco and didn't experience any racial discrimination. In Memphis, the situation was much different, both in the neighborhood and at school. Our boys, however, dealt with the discrimination much better than our daughter. Boys tend to bond and develop friendship and respect based on athletic skills and abilities. Our youngest son, Nelson Joseph, became friends with a classmate who lived in the neighborhood. The two boys played together at school, but the boy's mother would not allow them to play together in the neighborhood. However, before we left Memphis, the boy's mother had a softening of the heart, and the boys were permitted to play together in the neighborhood.

Unfortunately, our daughter, Janet had a very different experience. She was humiliated and rejected by the girls in school and on the playground. The girls wouldn't eat, talk, or play with her. She was left all alone. My wife arranged a transfer for Janet to the school where she was a teacher on staff.

As a family, we were actively involved in the spiritual life at Avery Chapel African Methodist Episcopal Church in Memphis. My wife and I sang in the choir and our children participated in children's activities and programs. We met several prominent African American leaders and became friends with one of the community leaders. After Sunday church service, we would drive to South Haven, Mississippi, to have lunch at the Piccadilly Cafeteria.

During this time, I was an avid golfer but couldn't play at the neighborhood golf course because of discrimination; I had to drive to South Memphis and play at a course in a predominantly black neighborhood. I also enjoyed watching the Professional Golfers' Association tournaments. Each year, the FedEx St. Jude Classic, a tournament on the PGA tour, is held in Memphis. One year, while watching the tournament as a spectator, I observed an evil spirit at work when a little boy picked up a black tournament player's ball and moved it behind a tree.

Memphis is the second largest city in the state of Tennessee, with a population of approximately seven hundred thousand. During the '60s, the city was the center of civil rights action. In 1968, it was the scene of a major strike by sanitation workers, and on April 4 of that year, Dr. Martin Luther King Jr. was assassinated by a lone sniper at the Lorraine Motel.

Yet, Memphis is also well known for its cultural contribution and that includes African Americans. Some of the renowned black musicians grew up in and around Memphis including Muddy Waters, B.B. King, Al Green and W.C. Handy.

ADMINISTRATIVE GRADUATE TRAINING

I consistently maintained my determination, commitment, and discipline to continue acquiring knowledge and skills through education. As I advanced in the military, my assignments became more diverse and required more focus on administration and management, I realized I needed more manage- ment training.

While in Washington State between 1970 and 1972, I took graduate level business classes at Pacific Lutheran University in Tacoma. In 1974, when I was reassigned to the Letterman Army Medical Center at the Presidio of San Francisco, I took classes at the University of San Francisco.

Then, in 1976 and 1982, I applied to the School of Business at California State University in Fresno. Despite all my preparation, however, my application was denied. I thought this was unfair and without merit and registered my protest by sending a letter in January 1983 to the Division of Graduate Studies and Research to request an appeal of the decision. They responded that my

Graduate Management Admission Test score was low and out of date (I was tested in 1977). When that door closed, however, another door opened.

I always search for alternative options when I encounter setbacks, barriers, and opposition. To obtain a much-needed graduate administrative degree, I decided to pursue a master's degree in public administration. At that point, I reset my strategy to overcome barriers and stumbling blocks and turned opposition into opportunity.

I applied and was accepted to the master's Public Administration Program at California State University, Long Beach, and was able to take my classes at California State University in Fresno. In 1982, I received the master's degree in Public Administration from the California State University. As a result of this achievement, and my faith, commitment and perseverance were strengthened.

PROFESSIONAL CERTIFICATE IN GERONTOLOGY

My desire to become trained in gerontology grew from a difficult working situation I experienced when I was hired as the director of a senior services department at St. Jude Medical Center, Fullerton, California. Without any previous experience working with seniors, I quickly recognized I was not qualified to serve as the director. So, I enrolled in a one-year gerontology program at the California State University in Fullerton. This helped me gain insight and increase my awareness of issues that affected seniors as they aged.

The study of gerontology is a multidisciplinary approach that includes the fields of biology, physiology, psychology, and sociology. The one-year training program focused on the physical, social, and mental changes individuals face as they age; this included age-related diseases, risk factors and elder abuse. My goal as the senior services director was to help the senior population served by the program at Jude Medical Center maintain the best quality of life.

CONFLICT RESOLUTION CERTIFICATE

I always have had a great interest in acquiring new skills and learning more about things, and my thirst for knowledge and experiences in life propelled that learning.

While I was serving on the Riverside County civil grand jury, I became interested in developing conflict resolution skills and so I enrolled in online mediation training. I learned how to focus on my clients' strengths rather than weaknesses, and how to use those strengths to move toward a resolution.

Afterwards, I went to the Institute for Advanced Dispute Resolution in Boulder, Colorado, for three days of practical training to reinforce the skills I'd learned. The training was practice-based and focused on solving problems and making decisions through a facilitative process; it was challenging. I successfully passed the program and received a mediation certificate. My goal was to get a job with Riverside County to help landlords and tenants resolve conflicts. However, I found out a that person in Riverside County without legal train- ing could not provide conflict resolution services for compensation; however, I could work as a volunteer.

CHAPTER 5
My Life Partner

At Central State, upper-class students traditionally initiate incoming freshman students. The initiation was designed as a fun activity. In 1954, during incoming freshman orientation and initiation week, new students were restricted from walking on the sidewalk near the cafeteria. They had to walk in the street.

One attractive, feisty young lady from Kentucky (the Blue Grass State) refused to comply with the upper-class students' request. She was quick to let them know that no one could tell her what to do. I became interested in this young lady and wanted to get to know her better. Her name was Peggy. During my second year, I developed a friendship with Peggy. I was also impressed with Peggy because her father drove her to the campus in a Chrysler New Yorker. Even though we dated others for a while, our relationship became more serious during my third year. On weekends, we would take long walks from Wilberforce to nearby communities of Xenia (four miles away) and Yellow Springs (eight miles). We continued to spend quality time with each other at Jack's Restaurant, a favorite off-campus student hangout.

Peggy was a member of the Delta Sigma Theta sorority and a Kappa Alpha Psi Sweetheart. I was a member of the Omega Psi Phi fraternity. Peggy's aca- demic concentration was in social work, while I followed a pre-medicine cur- riculum. As the relationship became more serious, I began to think about mar- riage. During my senior year and Peggy's third year, we became engaged, and I went to Lexington, Kentucky, to meet with her parents, Dewey, and Rebecca Jackson, to get their approval. Both parents gave their consent, with the stipula- tion that Peggy had to complete her college education.

We were married on August 25, 1957, at St. Paul African Methodist Episcopal Church in Lexington, where Peggy's family were active members and held leadership positions. Several of our college classmates and friends participated in the wedding ceremony. A good friend and fraternity brother from Connecticut served as my best man; Peggy's sister, Bessie Mae, was the maid of honor.

The summer I went to reserve officer training at Fort Bragg, Uncle Charles and Aunt Amanda adopted two young boys. After the wedding, Peggy and I could not afford a honeymoon, but we took a short romantic getaway to Cleveland, my home resident state. While there, we met the two playful young boys who had fun teasing us. In September 1957, I went to Iowa State University , to begin graduate studies; Peggy returned to Central State for one semester to complete her course work and spend one semester in Lexington for social service field work training. I've often wondered why we chose to get married and spend the first year of our marriage in different states. Perhaps our emotional bonds were strong enough to bridge the distance.

CHAPTER 6
Military Service Career

After I earned a bachelor's degree in chemistry, I planned to seek employment in the industrial sectors. During my summer vacation in 1957, I returned to Cleveland and tested job opportunities by applying to several industrial and auto parts manufacturing companies that were hiring chemistry graduates. I was rejected by every company to which I applied, without receiving any reason or explanation. Even with the bachelor's degree, I was unable to find a job in Cleveland's industrial sector. The rejection represented another example of my struggles as a black American living in a segregated society—opportunities and privileges went primarily to white people. Once again, I was determined to turn opposition into opportunity.

After I realized that gaining employment in the industrial sectors would not be successful, I needed to find an alternate pathway to support my wife. Therefore, I chose to begin my two years of obligated active military service and consider a military career. In 1948, President Truman had abolished racial discrimination in the armed forces. I viewed President Truman's decision as encouraging news and felt that a military career would offer the best opportunity for a comfortable lifestyle in America's segregated society. On June 30, 1958, I reported as a second lieutenant to the Army Medical Service School at Brooke Army Medical Center to begin active military training.

Brooke Army Medical Center is one of several military installations located in San Antonio, home of the Alamo Mission, one of the attractions we visited when we lived there in 1958 and 1965. The other military installations include Lockland Air Force Base, Randolph Air Force Base and Fort Sam Houston.

Upon entering on active duty, I had a twofold goal: serve my obligated two-year military duty and pursue a twenty-year military career. Fortunately, the army found a match with my education and military needs, and assigned me a major occupational specialist as chemist in the Army Medical Service Corps. Later, my occupation would change to biochemist.

The Medical Service Corps has two primary functions. First, it provides administrative officers the opportunity to manage various aspects of combat health support. Second, the corps provides allied science officers, who directly affect the health of the soldiers serving in the U.S. Army, as well as their families. The Medical Service Corps prepares its officers to be at the forefront of health care and provides them with excellent opportunities for advanced master's and doctorate degrees.

I was especially interested in this benefit and wanted to pursue a master's degree in biochemistry. I was placed into the medical allied sciences classification, which included biochemistry, microbiology, parasitology, immunology, clinical laboratory, and blood bank officer.

Once my training was complete, I was assigned to the 406th Medical General Laboratory in Camp Zama, Japan, reporting December 2, 1958. My wife and I traveled to Japan in a military ship sailing from Seattle, Washington, on November 22. The goal of completing a twenty-year military career would be a challenge because of my status as a reserve officer. A regular army commission status, however, would allow me to complete twenty years of active military service and receive retirement benefits.

As a reserve officer, I had no assurance of being retained on active duty after completing my two years of active military service. In fact, I could be released for any one of the following reasons: forced reduction in army strength, pass over for promotion, failure to meet acceptable standards of efficiency or conduct, and failure to meet standards prescribed for probationary officers. With hope and faith in God, I was willing to take the risk that I would achieve my goal. As my favorite scripture states, "I can do all things through Christ who strengthens me."

I submitted applications twice to the army for reclassification to a regular army commission status once in November 1958 and again in October 1959.

Neither application received favorable consideration. The response was that the applications did not indicate a lack of suitable qualifications but that other applicants were deemed better qualified. I felt I was denied the opportunity to obtain a regular army commission without any definitive information regarding the required qualifications.

Throughout most of my military career, I had limited social relationships with white families. However, in Japan, we had a close relationship with several white families. In fact, one family kept our children while we went to a party. I believed as Americans in Japan, we all felt displaced and accepting someone of a different ethnicity presented less risk there than in the United States.

The obstetrician who delivered our three bundles of joy was a close friend and adviser. We were the youngest couple in the laboratory and in our social circle. At work, most of the civilian employees and active-duty military personnel I supervised were either white or Asian. I didn't have the opportunity to work with or receive performance evaluations from any African American officers.

Despite the difficulties I encountered, I made steady progress and received significant expressions of praise—including a certificate of achievement; letter of appreciation; two army commendation medals for displaying the highest degree of proficiency, enthusiasm, and personal excellence in the performance of assigned duties. In 1970, I was also awarded a master's degree in biochemistry from the University of Tennessee. I felt my accomplishments were clear evidence of a good track record for future promotions and, therefore, expected to complete a twenty-year military career.

The average time for promotion from major to lieutenant colonel is between five to seven years. According to army promotion guidelines, my advancement was on target. In two years of service, I attained the grade of second lieutenant; in six years, captain; and within ten years, major. My earliest opportunity to be considered for promotion to lieutenant colonel was in 1973 after fifteen years of service.

Military life exceeded my expectations. It had a profound effect on me personally, and on my family and my career. I began my military career at a time in American history when black Americans were treated as inferior and white Americans did not believe that Jefferson's famous words—that all men are created equal—applied to black Americans. After discrimination in the military was abolished, conditions on military installations were much better than in the surrounding local communities. The military life sheltered us from some of the practices in the surrounding community.

Our children were born in a military hospital in Japan and, as a family, we traveled extensively, crossing from coast to coast and back again more than eight times on military reassignments and visiting family and friends. I enjoyed life on the military installations because of the variety and abundance of activities, entertainment, health care access, and children program that were available without any overt discrimination. Our children were excited to move from place to place because of the new family activities we would explore.

CHAPTER 7
Military Assignment

My military service chronicles more than seventeen years of active military service for my country in locations both domestic and international.

Dates	Location	Service titles
1958	Fort Sam Houston, Texas	Basic Military Training
1958–1962	Camp Zama, Japan	Chemist, 406th Medical Laboratory
1962–1965	Fort Sill, Oklahoma	Clinical Laboratory Manager, U.S. Army Hospital
1966	Fort Sam Houston, Texas	Advanced Military Training
1966–1967	Qui Nhon, Vietnam	Administrative Officer, 528th Medical Laboratory

1967–1968	Presidio, San Francisco	Chief of Chemistry, Letterman Army Hospital
1968–1970	Memphis, Tennessee	Graduate School, University of Tennessee
1970–1974	Fort Lewis, Washington	Chief of Chemistry, Madigan Army Medical Center
1974–1975	Presidio, San Francisco	Chief of Chemistry, Letterman Army Medical Center

BASIC MEDICAL SERVICE CORPS OFFICER MILITARY TRAINING

On June 30, 1958, I started my military service career by attending a four-month medical services corps officer orientation course at the Brooke Army Medical Center, San Antonio, Texas. New Medical Service Corps officers are required to attend the basic military training program, which includes a variety of courses:

- Military justice, which is the body of laws and procedures governing members of the armed forces; the Geneva Convention, which defined the basic rights of wartime prisoners, civilians, and military personnel; established protections for the wounded and sick; and established protections for civilians in and around war zones.
- Chemical, biological, and radiological warfare
- Emergency medical care
- Code of conduct, which is an ethics guide and U.S. Department of Defense directive to members, addressing an important U.S. military doctrine and tradition on how to evade capture, resist while a prisoner or escape from the enemy
- Behind enemy lines
- Land mine warfare
- Management of mass casualties

I ranked in the top third of the basic military training course with a grade average of eight-five. I was issued a certificate of completion and my military duty assignment to the 406th Medical General Laboratory in Camp Zama, Japan.

VISITING FAMILY AND FRIENDS AFTER BASIC TRAINING

I bought my first automobile, a 1954 Ford four-door sedan, in San Antonio. I was the first member in my family to own a car. I did not have any previous driving experience, but I believed I could drive.

I asked my friend and fellow college classmate to go with me to purchase the car. In fact, my friend drove the car off the dealer's lot to the base. After passing the written portion of the Texas driver's test, I failed the road portion because I didn't know how to back up—as I backed up, I didn't keep the car in my lane but crossed over into the oncoming lane. Immediately the officer had me return to the station and informed me I had violated the law and failed. I could return another day. I became concerned about driving the car back to the base without a driver's license. So much for thinking I knew how to drive just by watching someone else do it. Other interesting incidents occurred involving the car. One night after Peggy's arrival, I drove to the base theater and received a citation from the military police for parking in a non-parking zone. Of course, I sent Peggy to the office to clear the claim. Fortunately, the notice was an advisory warning.

After the basic training course graduation ceremony, all my fellow graduates and I were excited to go visit family and friends before reporting to our first military duty assignment. I was assigned to the 406th Medical General Laboratory at Camp Zama in Japan. Peggy and I departed San Antonio in our newly acquired 1954 Ford sedan to visit family in Georgia, Tennessee, and Kentucky. We stopped in New Orleans, Louisiana where we had motel reservations.

As young inexperienced drivers, we had no idea of the distance or estimated driving time from San Antonio to New Orleans. Consequently, we drove the rest of the afternoon of my departure day, all night and early the next day before arriving in New Orleans. During the night while Peggy was driving, she had a frightful experience. She was tired and began to see things on the highway that weren't there. At one point, she thought the car couldn't get over a bridge when in fact the road was flat. We stopped and changed drivers. I continued driving until we arrived at our destination.

We arrived in New Orleans exhausted; we needed sleep. Without knowing there were two motels with the same name along the highway, one serving white customers and the other African Americans, Peggy, who is fair-complexioned, went to the clerk at the first motel.

She was greeted by an older white man who asked in a demeaning tone, "Aren't you colored?"

"Yes," she answered.

"You need to go down the street to the colored motel," he said.

The building and surrounding area of the white motel was of course much nicer than the accommodations for black Americans. In New Orleans, we expe- rienced legalized discrimination based on the law that defined black Americans as non-citizens in America.

After a day of rest (in the other motel), we continued the trip to Columbus, Georgia, to visit Uncle Booker and see my family in Chattanooga; then, it was on to visit with Peggy's parents in Lexington. We remained in Lexington until it was time to drive to Seattle where we would board a military ship to Japan. Before going to Japan, Peggy and I had to get immunized for smallpox, typhoid, typhus, cholera, and yellow fever.

TRIP TO THE SEATTLE WASHINGTON SEAPORT

Even though we'd gained some highway driving experience in October on the trip from San Antonio to Lexington, our skills had not yet been tested on ice- slick highways. On November 15, 1958, we started our trip from Lexington to Seattle. The winter driving conditions were treacherous and challenging, and we encountered snow and ice on the highway.

U.S. Route 30 took us through Ohio, Indiana, Illinois, Iowa, and Nebraska. In Nebraska, I purchased and mounted tire chains to get through the snow and ice. As a first-time user of tire chains, I didn't know to remove the chains once there was no longer heavy snow and ice on the highway, and the chains broke.

As we continued on our trip , we passed through Wyoming, Montana, and Yakima, Washington, passed by Mount Rainier and into Seattle. We were traveling in American history when discrimination against African Americans was the norm. We were not granted equal access to hotels, motels, restaurants, and other public facilities. As black persons, we were not treated as human beings created by God, but rather as persons that were inferior to the privileged white class. In the southern states, once again we could not receive table service in a restaurant; we had to order takeout and pick it up at the rear of the restau- rant. We found greater hospitality at restaurants in the western states, but not at the motels.

Finding motel accommodations was frustrating and demoralizing. In general, Innkeepers were hesitant or outright refused to accommodate us. This happened in every state in which we stopped. Even when an illuminated motel sign clearly indicated a vacancy, the desk clerk would tell us there was no avail- ability. Some motel clerks pretended to be helpful and offered to notify another motel along our route. It took us a while to realize that the clerk was notifying the other motel that a black couple was coming. We were astonished when one motel clerk asked to see proof of our marital status. Of course, that didn't make sense for people traveling by automobile from state to state.

Despite the demeaning treatment, through faith and perseverance, we suc- cessfully arrived in Seattle on November 20, 1958, two days before our sched- uled departure date.

TRANSPACIFIC CRUISE EXPERIENCE

We boarded the USS General William Mitchell, a navy transport ship, in Seattle, for a thirteen-day transatlantic cruise to Yokohama, Japan. The ship transported military personnel their personal equipment, and automobiles. Accommodations for officers and their families were located on the upper decks while non-commissioned personnel were on the lower decks.

As first-time cruisers, we didn't know what to expect, and Peggy became anxious when she could no longer see land. In 1958, cruising on the Pacific Ocean onboard a military vessel during the winter was a unique and frightful experience. During the thirteen-day crossing, our ship encountered typhoons and experienced navigational and radar challenges. During the height of one storm, Peggy became so sick she could barely eat anything. The movement was awful. At one point, I was seated at the dining table when suddenly everything on the table began sliding and landed on the floor. When I could no longer deal with the tossing and turning, I returned to my cabin. We thankfully arrived at the Yokohama port on December 4, 1958.

MY JAPANESE EXPERIENCE

Upon arriving in Yokohama, we were transported to Camp Zama and assigned temporary housing until a family housing unit became available. Four days later, we received keys to a one-bedroom house in the Sagamihara family housing complex about three miles from Camp Zama. This family housing was provided for military families as well as families of American civilians who worked for the army. Facilities and activities available at Sagamihara included a commissary, a gas station, a convenience store, several parks for children, a pool that was open seasonally, tennis courts, a gym, and an elementary school. My responsibilities as chief of the chemistry department included managing scientific testing and analysis performed by Japanese scientist and assigned military personnel. The 406th Medical General Laboratory served as the central laboratory for the Far East. The laboratory began operations at Yokohama in 1946. Other departments at the laboratory included epidemiology, bacteriology, serology, veterinary medicine, and pathology.

As the main medical laboratory for the Far East command, the laboratory specialized in testing for opiates and other illegal drugs at army hospitals, as well as research on communicable diseases, especially the Korean hemorrhagic fever, which is caused by a virus that can result in kidney failure. It was endemic in Asia and especially in Korea. Additional laboratory testing was performed on food products that were distributed to the Republic of Korea troops. In November 1961, I served six days of temporary duty at the Okinawa Station Hospital in connection with medical activities.

On January 24, 1962, I was issued temporary duty orders to Seoul and Taejon, Korea, to assist the Republic of Korea Army (the army of South Korea) in conducting a field survey for detecting preicteric and anicteric cases of hepatitis. The preicteric phase of hepatitis-A includes nausea, vomiting, fever, headache, and fatigue. Anicteric hepatitis usually has an absence of clinical jaundice or any yellowish discoloration of the skin or white of the eyes. My team included five soldiers and a veterinarian. Other temporary duty orders sent me to Taiwan and Okinawa.

In most military organizations, junior officers are assigned additional duties to increase their awareness of organizational responsibility so they can learn how to be responsible and administer services other than their primary duty. As the junior Medical Service Corps officer at the laboratory, I was assigned the additional duties of narcotic control officer; alternate air raid warden; member of the professional library committee; chemical, biological, and radiological officer; explosion ordnance reconnaissance officer; radiological safety officer; member of the junior program budget advisory group; and custodian of radiological material.

My experience in Japan was educational, interesting, and exciting. My wife and I gained a great appreciation for the Japanese culture and embraced it as much as possible. We took Japanese language lessons and learned to speak well enough to shop at the local market. Before World War II, golf was very popular, and it became a national pastime in later years after the war. In Japan, golf was not only a major activity for the Japanese but also a favorite activity for me and many other military officers. Working as a golf caddy in Chattanooga, I'd had limited exposure to golf; caddies played on Mondays when the course was closed to the public. I had some knowledge of how to play the game, but I didn't know the fundamentals of the golf swing. In Japan, I took golf lessons from a Japanese professional and later from a military sergeant on active military duty as a golf teaching professional. He was a good golfer who went on the win the 1969 U.S. Open in his only PGA tour and won other titles on the U.S. Senior Open Tour.

While in Japan, we started our family with Errol Allen as the first arrival on August 29, 1959. He was followed by his sister, Janet Lynn, on December 24, 1960, and their little brother, Nelson Joseph, on November 6, 1961.

On December 23, 1960, the night before Janet was born, Peggy was helping military wives decorate the officer's club for the annual Christmas party—Janet was born early the next morning.

Our grandparents were concerned when they received Errol's baby picture; he was wearing a kimono. Even though they were American born at Camp Zama Hospital, a military facility located on Japanese soil, our children were not yet considered full U.S. citizens. Upon return to the United States, they had to be issued birth certificates from the State Department.

We explored Japan by train and automobile. On a thirty-mile drive from Zama to Tokyo, we experienced heavy and fast-moving traffic, especially taxis. The other cities we visited included Yokohama, Kobe (home of Kobe meat, which is renowned for its flavor, tenderness, and marbled texture), Kyoto and Atsugi (the location of the Navy Exchange, an air naval station). Our longest trip by automobile was to Kyoto, which is located on the southern tip of the island, three-hundred miles from Camp Zama. The Kyoto trip was interesting and rewarding because the route passed through Hiroshima, the first city in history to be targeted by a nuclear weapon during World War II.

In Kyoto, we stayed at a Japanese hotel and slept on a Japanese platform bed, a low-profile bed made of solid wood, with tatami mats laid on top as a mattress.

RETURN TO AMERICA

In the summer of 1962, I returned to the United States with Peggy and three products made in Japan: Errol, Janet, and Nelson Joseph. At that time, Errol was three years old, Janet was two and Nelson Joseph was one. Anyone traveling with three small children should realize that assistance from both parents and sometimes other passengers is required. But I was first lieutenant, an officer, and a gentleman, and thought too highly of myself. Therefore, I did not assist my wife with the children on their first airplane trip. Instead, I relied on other lower-rank military personnel who graciously assisted.

Our family departed Japan from Tachikawa Air Base on a military aircraft powered by a Douglas DC-6, a piston engine built by Douglas Aircraft Company in Southern California. We stopped over in Oahu, Hawaii, for four days at Fort DeRussy (now the Hale Koa Hotel), an armed forces recreation center on Waikiki near the Hawaiian Hilton Resort. One day, Janet, our adventurous daughter, waded into the Pacific Ocean. My wife screamed and we both ran to get her.

After getting Janet safely out of the ocean, we had a big laugh and enjoyed the remainder of the vacation. At the end of our Hawaiian vacation, we boarded another military flight to Travis Air Force Base in Fairfield, California, where we picked up our automobile for the drive to Lexington, Kentucky, and Chattanooga, Tennessee, to show the children to their grandparents and other family members.

In Japan there was a high demand for American four door sedans manufactured between 1950-1960. Many military personnel going to Japan during those years became aware of the opportunity and took automobiles they intended to sell before leaving Japan, I sold my 1954 Ford four door Sedan at a premium price and purchased a Peugeot., a small stick-shift four-door sedan manufactured in France.

I picked up my vehicle at Fairfield Air Force Base and began the long trip to Chattanooga and Lexington. We started the trip in Fairfield with three small children and thirteen pieces of luggage. Unfortunately, there was no family member available to give guidance on how to pack and travel by car with small children. As a young family that had been out of the United States for four years, we packed enough clothing for the entire trip. It didn't occur to me that laundromats were available along the way for washing clothes. Each night that we stopped for lodging, I removed luggage from the trunk and the top-mounted luggage rack. The following morning, the luggage had to be placed back on top of the luggage rack and in the trunk.

The trip went without incident until the car broke down on a Sunday morning in Colorado about one hundred fifty miles from the nearest repair shop; of course, repair shops were closed on Sunday. Several motorists stopped and helped, but they had no knowledge of a French manufactured automobile and neither did I. Unfortunately, my automotive and mechanical skills were weak. But somehow, "God made a way." I gained enough insight and resolved the issue, and we got back on the road.

We were amazed at some of the improvements in travel for African Americans compared to the conditions we'd experienced four years earlier in 1958 when we traveled to Seattle. We observed that restaurant and motel clerks displayed a greater degree of acceptance and hospitality.

U.S. ARMY HOSPITAL, FORT SILL, OKLAHOMA

My first stateside duty assignment was to serve as the chief of the clinical laboratory in the pathology department at the U.S. Army Hospital at Fort Sill, Oklahoma which is located near the community of Lawton. In this assignment, I provided technical supervision for specimen testing, supervising civilian and assigned military personnel; diagnostic consultation; operations management; and ensuring compliance with federal regulatory requirements and national accreditation standards.

While at Fort Sill, I received promotion to captain and was awarded the Army Commendation Medal for Meritorious Service for the period of August 1, 1964, to August 1, 1965.

When I reported with my family to Fort Sill, in 1962, we were assigned tem- porary housing in the officer's quarters. We were eligible for a three-bedroom house, but long-term family housing wasn't available, and I was directed to seek private housing in the city of Lawton. Lawton is in Southwestern Oklahoma. The population in Lawton was approximately sixty-two thousand. Even though Fort Sill was founded in 1901 and provided economic and population stabil- ity, there was still widespread housing discrimination. We were shown rental housing in the Lawton communities that was unsanitary, in deplorable con- dition or located in undesirable and unsafe areas. As an officer in the United States Army, I refused to accept substandard living conditions for my family; therefore, our family remained in the officer's temporary housing for two weeks until the housing office found something suitable on the military base.

Finally, housing was provided in the old hospital buildings that had been converted to family housing. I was given paint and supplies to decorate the walls to meet our color preferences. I felt it would be better and safer to live in sub-standard housing on the military installation rather than in the city of Lawton, and it was more convenient to my workplace.

About two years later, in 1964, I was advised that the building we lived in would be demolished. Three-bedroom units on the military installation were still unavailable. Again, I was advised to look for private housing in the city of Lawton. Fortunately, conditions for black American military personnel had improved, and I successfully rented a house in a mixed neighborhood near a back gate to the installation. The children continued to attend school on the military installation.

Peggy's major at Central State had been social welfare, but she was accepted as a substitute teacher in Lawton Unified School District. The principal was so impressed with her teaching style and classroom management that he recommended she take education courses at a community college. Peggy enrolled at the Chickasha Community College, which was about forty miles away, to obtain her teaching credentials. During the rest of our stay in Lawton, Peggy worked as an elementary school teacher.

In Lawton, teachers' cars are required to have Oklahoma license plates. I entered on active duty from my home state of Ohio and our car had Ohio tags. To meet this requirement, we purchased a second car, an old Chrysler DeSoto. The car rumbled and rocked when driven. Fortunately, Peggy only had a short distance to drive to her school. Before leaving Lawton, I traded our Peugeot sedan for a 1960 Mercedes Benz sedan, a car seldom seen in the '60s.

Sometimes my youth convinced me unwisely to try to do the impossible. While assigned to the hospital at Fort Sill, I received temporary orders to go to Walter Reed Army Medical Center in Washington, DC for special training. I decided to drive my newly acquired Mercedes to Washington, DC, one thousand forty miles and an estimated driving time of twenty-one hours. I had three days to get there. On day one, I made great time and arrived in Springfield, Ohio (nine hundred fifty-eight miles), around 1:00 p.m. I stopped and had lunch with a friend and fellow college classmate and continued my trip.

I still had an additional four hundred sixty-four miles to go, which would take at least six hours. I realized I couldn't physically make the rest of the trip without another driver. God was with me. While driving through Columbus, I passed a young, uniformed military soldier hitchhiking. I circled back and asked, "Where are you going"? he said "Baltimore, Maryland.

I offered to give this total stranger (my first and last hitchhiker) a ride to his destination if he could drive a Mercedes Benz. We drove the remainder of the day and early into the next one. We arrived at his destination in Baltimore at 4:00 a.m. Then I drove to my hotel in Washington, DC, but did not sleep as I didn't want to take the chance of oversleeping and missing my class. I am thankful that God protected me in this situation. Even though I trusted another military person with my life, the incident was crazy and dangerous.

BROOKE ARMY MEDICAL CENTER

In July 1965, I returned to the Brooke Army Medical Center to attend advanced military training. Career Medical Service Corps officers are required to take this training, which usually occurs within six to seven years of active military duty. The nine months course dates were September 12, 1965 – May 20, 1966. This training consisted of army policy and procedures, map training, physical training, and weapon training. I successfully completed the advanced training program and received assignment orders to Vietnam.

Before going to Vietnam in July 1966, I relocated my family to Lexington, the city where Peggy's parents and sister lived. We bought a three-bedroom house with financial assistance from Peggy's father. The children attended public school in Lexington and worshipped services at St. Paul African Methodist Episcopal Church. My nephew Gary Lowery from Chattanooga lived with the family in Lexington for one year. Peggy was successful in getting a teaching position with the Lexington Unified School District.

QUY NHON, VIETNAM

I departed from Travis Air Force Base, California on a military-leased aircraft with other military personnel. My flight made stops at Guam (the United States island territory in Micronesia), and Tachikawa, Japan. Passengers were not allowed to deplane at either destination. Upon arrival in Saigon, Vietnam, I was transported on a C-130 military aircraft to Quy Nhon, a coastal city in central Vietnam. During my tour of duty, the commercial activities of the city focused on agriculture and fishing.

I was assigned as the administrative officer at the 528th Medical Detachment. This detachment was a field-type laboratory that provided testing of patient biological fluids and performed autopsies. The 528th Medical Detachment also served as the blood distribution center for the sector. Blood delivered to the unit was distributed to the adjacent 85th Evacuation Hospital and other field hospitals in Pleiku and An Khê. My commanding officer was a physician with a specialty in pathology, who was serving his obligated time for receiving financial assistance from the army while in medical school. My unit was attached to the 55th Medical Group for support and adjacent to the 85th Evacuation Hospital.

My principal duties were as biochemist and other duties were as delegated by my commanding officer. As the biochemist, I supervised the clinical laboratory, verified the calibration accuracy of testing equipment and reviewed laboratory test results. My administrative and property book officer responsibilities included signing for the unit's property, checking inventory, and other adminis- trative duties as delegated by my commanding officer.

One of my responsibilities was to ensure proper calibration and operation of laboratory equipment at satellite medical units in Pleiku, An Khê and Vũng Tàu. I traveled by military aircraft (C-130 or helicopter) to the various destina- tions to perform my duties. The Viet Cong launched the 1966 Tet Offensive while I was at a satellite medical unit in Pleiku; I was grounded at the facility for forty-eight hours.

The most risky, and dangerous action I took was driving my unit's jeep on a sixty mile trip from Quy Nhon to Pleiku. The route took us through a moun- tain pass where military convoys were frequently ambushed. My only weapon was a 45-caliber pistol. Even though I joined the military convoy traveling through the mountains, there was great risk. The purpose of the trip was to visit with fellow classmates from my advanced training program at Brooke Army Medical Center for a cookout and fellowship. I was blessed that everything went well. After six months in the war zone, I was approved for one week of rest and recuperation in Hawaii. During that vacation, Peggy joined me in Oahu, Hawaii, while my mother kept the children.

On February 19, 1967, I was admitted to the 85th Evacuation Hospital with a diagnosis of viral hepatitis inflammation of the liver and was discharged on March 9. Hepatitis is most often caused by a virus. At that time, the type of hepatitis was not specified.

Before going to Vietnam, I met with the chief of the Medical Service Corps to express my interest in pursuing a master's degree in biochemistry. I was advised to apply to the university of my choice. Once my Vietnam tour of duty (July 1966 to July 1967), I was awarded the Army Commendation Medal (1st oak leaf cluster) for my Vietnam service and was approved for long-term school- ing. Unfortunately, budget space was not available for 1967. However, the army reassured me that I would go to graduate training in 1968 by issuing two set of assignment orders in 1967.The first set of orders assigned me to Letterman Army Medical Center, Presidio of San Francisco for one year. The second set of orders was approval to attend graduate training at the University of Tennessee, Memphis in September 1968.

It was essential for me, as an active-duty officer in a technical or professional discipline to a to have a master's degree in my area of specialization. In general, biochemists are responsible for the planning and execution of clinical labora- tory testing, medical research and development, forensic toxicology, and drug testing. World military assignments may include section, branch, department or division chief at various medical centers, hospitals, and drug testing laborato- ries and in the deployment environment.

MY FIRST EXPERIENCE AT THE PRESIDIO OF SAN FRANCISCO

The Presidio was the center for defense of the Western United States during World War II. It was also home of the Letterman Army Medical Center, which included the hospital and a separate research facility. The Presidio was closed in 1995 and then managed by the Presidio Trust, a U.S. government corporation that was established by Congress in 1996.

Before reporting to Letterman General Hospital at the Presidio, I went to Lexington to see my family and arranged for them to move to San Francisco. I had not seen my wife in six months and my children in a year. Errol was eight, Janet was seven and little Nelson Joseph was six. We retained ownership of the house we'd purchased and leased it to a young family. Then, we started our trip from Lexington to San Francisco by automobile. Since the passage of the *Civil Rights Act* of 1964, which ended segregation in public places and banned dis- crimination based on race, color, religion, sex, or national origin, traveling by automobile was now more enjoyable and fun.

The children were dressed in shorts and tee shirts—summer attire. Along the route, we stopped at rest stops for restroom breaks and children's play time. When we reached Sacramento, the temperature was nearly one hundred degrees, and the car air conditioner was going full blast. On arrival in San Francisco the temperatures were in the sixties. We learned that in San Francisco, the summer and winter temperatures are reversed. We were so uncomfortable in summer attire that our first stop was to the military post exchange to pur- chase long pants and jackets.

Our next stop was the military guest house, where we received temporary accommodations. While at the guest house, the children chose to play in the family car, which was unlocked and parked behind the guest house. Behind the guest house was a hill. One of our children released the emergency brake and the car rolled backward and hit the retaining wall. Fortunately, no one was hurt and the car only experienced minor damage. Of course, the children could not recall who was responsible.

I was eligible for a three-bedroom house but was informed by the housing office it would be six months before a unit would become available. We were advised to rent a house in a nearby community in Marin County. We rented a house in San Rafael California for six months before moving to military housing on the Presidio. Along the backyard was the fairway of the Presidio Golf and Country Club; a challenging course, which my son Errol and I played occasionally.

At that time, we only had one car and now I was commuting about fifteen miles one way to the hospital. After Peggy was hired as an elementary school teacher in the Novato School District in Novato, we needed a second car. Which provided me an opportunity to get a long desired sports car. I purchased a TR 250, an appealing roadster that was a rugged, powerful English-manufactured sports car. I enjoyed the exciting, thrilling, and exhilarating driving experience up and down the Waldo Grade curves on Highway 101 and crossing the Golden Gate Bridge daily on my commute from San Rafael and the Presidio.

On this assignment, San Francisco became my favorite city because of its character, exquisite diversity, charm, challenging hills, excitement, and environment. Presidio was an extraordinary place to live. After moving to the Presidio, Peggy and I reversed our commuting roles. Peggy was now commuting from the Presidio to Novato five days a week. We only lived a short distance from the Golden Gate Bridge, which made her commute easier.

MADIGAN ARMY MEDICAL CENTER

After completing my graduate training, I received assignment to Madigan Army Medical Center, Fort Lewis, Washington, with a reporting date of October 20, 1970. Before going to Madigan, I received military orders to attend a six-week special training course for Allied Science Medical Service officers at Walter Reed Army Medical Center in Washington, D.C.

At Madigan, I served as chief of chemistry in the department of pathology. I met several professional African American military officers including a pharmacist and two physicians. This was one of my favorite military assignments. Madigan is located at Fort Sill and close to McCord Airforce Base nine miles from the city of Tacoma. As a regional medical center, Madigan serves the medical and emergency care needs to over one hundred thousand retirees and their families who live in Washington and portions of California. My wife and I were socially active in Tacoma and Lakewood. I was active with my fraternity, Omega Psi Phi, while Peggy was active with her sorority, Delta Sigma Theta. We formed a close relationship with a friendly, outgoing couple who lived in Renton. The wife was a librarian, and her husband was a schoolteacher. We were treated like family and attended numerous social and sport events with them. We also formed close bonds with a military family who lived in the neighborhood. This family had two sons, who were friends and playmates of our sons, Errol, and Nelson Joseph. After leaving active military service, they moved to Lithonia, Georgia. While on active duty, we shared many social events and family gatherings and have visited with them several times in Georgia.

With increased military promotions there would be greater emphasis placed on administrative responsibilities. I realized I needed to sharpen my management skills and, in 1971, began to pursue training in a Master of Business Administration program at Pacific Lutheran University in Tacoma. I started taking foundation courses before I could be enrolled in the advanced classes. Unfortunately, because of reassignment to San Francisco in 1974, I was unable to complete the program.

My oldest niece, Sheila Lowery, came to live with us to pursue a nursing career. She was accepted into nursing school at Pacific Lutheran University and graduated in 1978. My mother also came to visit with us in Tacoma. In 1974, when I received assignment orders to Letterman Army Medical Center at the Presidio of San Francisco, my mother and niece were still living with us.

RETURN TO THE CITY BY THE BAY

In 1974, the chief of pathology at Madigan Army Medical Center (a physician and colonel in the medical corps and my rating officer) invited me to transfer with him to Letterman Army Medical Center at the Presidio of San Francisco to serve as the chief of chemistry. This chief of pathology demonstrated a high level of confidence in my knowledge and past performance.

I was hoping this transfer would have a positive impact on the lieutenant colonel officers' promotion board that considered reserve active-duty candidates for promotion. Nonetheless, I was excited and thrilled to return to San Francisco; it was my favorite city.

My mother was still visiting with us, and she accompanied us on our automobile trip to San Francisco. My mother rode with me while the children rode in the other car with their mother. Shortly after arriving in San Francisco, my mother returned to Chattanooga. My niece Sheila moved into the city of Tacoma and continued her nursing training. She successfully completed the program and was awarded a Bachelor of Nursing degree in July 1978.

On this assignment to the Presidio, we established close relationships with two African American military families that lived on the Presidio: one family with two boys and another family with two girls. The couple with the two girls retired and live in Foster City. We attended many social outings and activities with each family. We went to dances and party events in the North Beach area of San Francisco and San Carlos.

We have maintained a long relationship with the family living in Foster City. Today, we live in Dublin, California, which is only a forty-five-minute drive from Foster City. After reconnecting with the family, we get together socially and communicate frequently by phone.

CHAPTER 8
Military Service Termination

Reserve officers on active military duty experience a two-tier promotion system. First, they are considered for promotion by an active-duty promotion board for reserve officers at each grade level. Second, they are considered for promotion by a reserve officer promotion board. In 1973 and 1974, my name was submitted to the Lieutenant Colonel Reserve Officers Promotion Board, which considers eligible reserve officers on active duty. I was not selected for promotion by either board because, as it was stated, my performance evaluations were significantly lower than my peers'.

It was frustrating, and I was perplexed as I had moved up the promotional ladder from second lieutenant to major within the prescribed time. However, snags occurred with consideration of my promotion from major to lieutenant colonel. It became apparent to me that I was being evaluated by a different set of standards. The inconsistency only occurred with the active-duty promotion of reserve officers. The perception was widely held by many white evaluators that an African American's best performance was just average and rarely superior, exceptional, or outstanding. In comparison with my contemporaries, my scores were lower, but they were accompanied by a strong narrative. However, only the numerical scores had an impact on promotion.

On November 19, 1973, I submitted an appeal of my efficiency report to the Department of the Army, Military Personnel in Alexandria, Virginia. In my appeal, I stressed how diligently I had worked and how I was extremely success- ful and had made significant contributions and innovations in my duty assign- ments but rarely received efficiency ratings equal to or above my white con- temporaries. I summarized my active-duty assignments and accomplishments, which included my service as chief of the chemistry section in the pathology department of various military hospitals and medical centers: United States Hospital, Fort Sill Hospital, Madigan Army Medical Center, Fort Lewis, Letterman Army Hospital and Letterman Army Medical Center at the Presidio. Even though my assignments were at different health care facilities, the mission and job responsibilities were basically the same: planning, verification of accu- racy testing of biological specimens, drug testing and forensic toxicology to support the physician's diagnosis and treatment plan for their patient.

Through my seventeen years and four months of service, I was innovative and made improvements at each duty assignment. Additionally, letters of support were sent to the board from the medical corps and Medical Service Corps officers', including from four colonels and four majors, attesting to my character and duty performance. The board response to the appeal was that the evidence presented did not justify withdrawing or altering the report.

Non-selection to lieutenant colonel was stressful and became a threat to end my military career. In 1974, I asked several of my past commanding officers, fellow officers, and associates to write to the promotion board on my behalf. My name was again submitted to the 1975 Reserve Officers Promotion Board for the third and final time. According to promotion policy, "a United State Army Reserve officer on active duty who has not been promoted to the next higher grade after three consecutive years will be released from active duty." I was not selected by the 1975 promotion board and, therefore, after seventeen years-and-two months on active duty I was released on October 17, 1975.

It's interesting to note that completing an additional eight months on active duty would have given me eighteen years, and I would have been allowed to stay to complete a twenty-year career.

CHAPTER 9
Promotion Board Lawsuit

When I was released from active military service, I lost my expected retirement benefits. I was devastated and demoralized. Now, I had entered a state of darkness in which my hopes and dreams of a successful military career were shattered. Moreover, I was angry, upset, and willing to fight, but I didn't have a strategy or know what to do. Nevertheless, I remained a member of the ready reserve with an obligation to serve two weeks on active military duty each year.

The premature end of my military career was the most difficult setback I'd ever experienced and the biggest challenge I had to overcome. I saw no clear path for restoration. I met and consulted with family members and friends who gave me advice and recommended a plan of action. My children's pediatrician advised me to pursue legal action. His recommendation gave me a ray of hope. I prayed and put my trust in God, and the support of family and friends was a tremendous help.

I navigated the state of darkness and unjustified termination by taking legal action against the United States Army; it was unprecedented, and it took great courage. In 1976, I filed a lawsuit against the United States Army Reserve Officers' Promotion Board, alleging that the board failed to follow the prescribed army policy for selected lieutenant colonels. On March 21, 1977, I joined as a plaintiff in a class action suit (Fisher v. Unites States) with other affected officers. We secured legal representation from a highly respected law firm in Baltimore, Maryland. Resolving the tedious matter took more than five years.

The first phase occurred on May 21, 1979. In that phase, the United States Court of Claims held that the original 1974 and 1975 Lieutenant Colonel

Reserve Officers Promotion Board recommendations were invalid but offered no permanent relief. Our legal team continued to fight for us and was successful in getting the court to reconsider its decision. On August 15, 1980, the Court entered an order granting judgement and ruling that the affected officers were entitled to return to active duty or receive constructive service credit to the extent required to complete twenty years of service, together with back pay. By the time of the settlement, my scheduled retirement date of June 30, 1978, had passed and I was now eligible for retirement.

On September 8, 1980, the United States Court of Claims ordered my release from active duty and established June 30, 1978, as my new release date, which was the same as my scheduled retirement date. On June 22, 1981, I received back pay and allowances to settle the judgement, and my military records were corrected to show retirement effective June 30, 1978.

Twenty-five days before my established retirement date, on June 5, 1978, I received promotion to lieutenant colonel from the reserve officer promotion board.

This action authorized me to retire in the highest grade held as a reserve officer. The judgement from the Court of Claims represented a significant accomplishment and a blessing because my twenty-year military career was restored.. Additionally, all retirement benefits were restored: medical care, dental care, military flights, commissary, and post-exchange shopping privileges.

CHAPTER 10
Health Care Career

During my season of uncertainty, difficulty and challenge, I decided to pursue a course of action that would minimize disruption to my wife and children. The children were in middle and high school in San Francisco. Peggy was an elementary school teacher in the Novato Unified School System. We stayed in San Francisco and leased a three-bedroom apartment on 19th Avenue in the Richmond District. Once the family was settled, I began to concentrate on my future.

While counting my blessings and reflecting on my strengths and attributes, I realized that God had a plan, a purpose, and a destiny for my life. The military had taught me discipline, self-confidence, and self-control, which I believe are all desirable attributes of good character. At the tender age of forty-one, I was young and energetic and had accomplished much in my life. I had earned a bachelor's degree in chemistry and a master's degree in biochemistry, attained the grade of major while on active duty, and served over seventeen years of active military service with one year in a Vietnam. I felt confident that the knowledge and skills I'd gained were more than sufficient to start a new career.

I thought a job in the health care industry would provide the best opportunity for growth and development for a long-term career. I began my job hunting by applying for an administrative position in the nuclear medicine department at the Madigan Army Medical Center in Lakewood, Washington. The department head was a physician whom I knew professionally and socially. I also applied for a laboratory manager position at St. Agnes Medical Center in Fresno. I was a little anxious and willing to accept the first position offered.

However, even though I was fascinated with the idea of owning a boat, living in Washington State was not my first choice because of the cool temperatures and long rainy season.

While waiting for responses from the two health care organizations, I received a conference call with three administrators from St. Agnes to discuss the employment offer. Without much hesitation, I accept the offer at St. Agnes. A few days later, Madigan also offered me the administrative position in the nuclear medicine department.

ST. AGNES MEDICAL CENTER CLINICAL LABORATORY

In August 1975, I was introduced to the Catholic Health Care Services at Saint Agnes Medical Center in Fresno. My position was the clinical laboratory manager. After one year at St. Agnes, I accepted a position in Flint, Michigan, as administrative manager for the Michigan Biomedical Laboratory.

However, I returned to Saint Agnes in 1979 and completed ten years of service. The Catholic health care brand is based on a holistic approach that treats the physical, emotional, and spiritual needs of each patient. As the laboratory manager, I was responsible for the management of laboratory personnel, technical equipment, and financial resources. My first order of business was to meet with each technologist to discuss their needs, ambitions, job duties and any issues that needed to be addressed. This helped me get to know the staff, and the staff could express their concerns to executive management. Besides my position, the laboratory also included medical technologist section team leaders for chemistry, serology, blood bank, microbiology, and pathology.

I was successful in improving the working conditions for technologists, arranging for section leaders to attend workshops to enhance their skills and installing new equipment. I also made a positive impact on the working environment, pay and recognition of technologists' achievements.

My family remained in San Francisco, and I rented an apartment near California State University. On Friday evening, I'd board a flight to San Francisco and return to Fresno Sunday afternoon. The flight to San Francisco became a social event because of the fellowship and association with other regular commuters who took the same flight each week.

In 1976, while attending a national laboratory conference in San Diego, I met Alfred Cook, an African American businessman and owner of the Michigan Biomedical Laboratory in Flint, Michigan. During our conversation, Alfred said he was looking for an administrative manager and I should contact him if I was interested. I discussed the option of remaining in my current position at St. Agnes or accepting a job in Flint and gaining business management experience. The benefits of moving would be a higher salary and a shorter driving distance to visit family in Kentucky and Tennessee.

MICHIGAN BIOMEDICAL LABORATORY

On August 23, 1976, I made an expenses-paid site visit to Michigan Biomedical Laboratory to see the facility, meet the staff and assess the administrative needs. On September 3, 1976, I was offered and accepted the position of administrative manager.

As administrative manager, my responsibilities included the following:

- Developing, long-range plans, and interpreting policies and procedures.
- Preparing budgets, and managing inventory.
- Directing personnel and supervising the technical areas in which I was certified.

This employment opportunity had an attractive salary with a fringe-benefit package that included vacation, sick leave, educational travel, family health insurance and life insurance.

Additional benefits included the relationship that my wife, Peggy, and I developed with Alfred and his wife (also an elementary school teacher). We attended many social events together. Alfred was an avid golfer and college football fan; University of Michigan was his favorite team. During the '70s, he attended all Rose Bowl games University of Michigan played in. In 1977, Alfred gave our family a fun-and-relaxation trip to Hilton Head, South Carolina, where he and I played several rounds of golf.

On October 14, 1976, my family started the trip from San Francisco to Flint by driving two cars—a Mercury sedan and a Fiat convertible—and we didn't encounter any snow or ice on the freeways. We purchased a beautiful two-story three-bedroom house with a full basement, an ideal place for indoor activities such as table tennis, board games, listening to music and social gathering during the long, hard winter months.

Shortly after arriving in Flint, we experienced our first major snowstorm, which was so severe we couldn't drive our car to the supermarket. So, we walked. It was only a distance of two blocks from the house, but on the walk home, the falling snow weakened the paper bags and all our groceries ended up falling into the snow.

During the winters of 1976 and 1977, we experienced severe cold weather with an abundance of snow. Each morning the children and I shoveled snow from the driveway to get to work and school. Errol and Janet were enrolled in Northern High School, and Nelson Joseph attended a middle school. When we returned at the end of the day, we had to shovel it a second time. On two occasions, a long, severe snowstorm hit the area and resulted in the schools closing—I still managed to get to work, but with difficulty. Our next-door neighbor was a friendly couple with one child. During one snowstorm, we got together and played board games and discussed buying and sharing a snowplow. Before that could happen, they decided to move to Tucson, Arizona.

The laboratory provided testing services for biological specimens submitted for analysis, such as blood and urine. Alfred obtained agreements from physicians' offices to provide a specimen pick-up service, test patients' biological fluids and deliver reports to the physician's office in a timely manner. Between 1977 and 1978, the laboratory experienced tremendous growth and relocated to a larger building. Alfred also purchased a small fleet of subcompact cars (Chevettes) that traveled up to one hundred miles one way to pick up specimens and deliver them to the laboratory.

Flint is located along the Flint River northwest of Detroit and is the largest city and county seat of Genesee County. In the '70s, Flint had a vibrant economy built around General Motors automobile manufacturing. We lived in Flint from December 1976 to January 1979. By the late '80s the city would sink into a deep economic depression after General Motors closed and demolished several factories in the area, the effects of which remain today.

In the spring of 1978, while I was still working at Michigan Biomedical Laboratory, I received a telephone call from the president and CEO at Saint Agnes Medical Center to express appreciation for my outstanding performance as the laboratory manager from 1975 to 1976 and to invite me to return. I was amazed that I was held in such high esteem. At that time, I declined the offer. A few weeks later, I received a second call from the St. Agnes CEO and a job offer for the position of consulting laboratory manager. The responsibility of this position was to resolve personnel issues and employee unrest in the clini- cal laboratory.

On April 6, 1978, I requested a temporary leave of absence from Michigan Biomedical Laboratory for a few months with the expectation of returning July 3. Alfred granted me the leave of absence, and I accepted a temporary position as laboratory consultant at St. Agnes. The timing of my departure was perfect because Michigan Biomedical Laboratory was experiencing cash flow issues and my relationship with Alfred was becoming rocky. On June 12, I advised Alfred in a Western Union mailgram that I was resigning my position at Michigan Biomedical Laboratory.

LABORATORY CONSULTANT AT ST. AGNES

I returned to St. Agnes Medical Center as a clinical laboratory consultant on a ninety-day contract. Upon arriving at St. Agnes, I met with the executive team to discuss personnel issues and unrest in the laboratory, the goals and expected outcomes. I was assigned the responsibility and authority to do whatever was necessary to restore stability.

I worked diligently with the laboratory staff, meeting with each employee individually on all shifts and in all specialty areas to determine their skill level and desired working conditions. Technologists were required to know how to operate sophisticated automated analytical instruments and make decisions about the validity of the data to be used by physicians in medical decisions. I evaluated the working environment; the status of the instruments, to determine if they needed to be upgraded and modernized; technologist training needs; and how exceptional performance in a particular area of expertise was recognized. I proposed establishing an advancement career ladder, providing technicians outside training opportunities, increasing compensation, and improving the management structure in the laboratory. I reported my recommendations to the executive administration, and the laboratory staff was pleased with the improvements that were implemented.

After successfully resolving the personnel matters, I was interested in finding permanent work within another medical center department. I recognized that there was limited opportunity for growth in the clinical laboratory field; I wanted diversity, growth, and increased compensation. The Chief Executive Officer at St. Agnes Medical Center offered me the opportunity to transfer to the planning department as a planning assistant, and this proved to be the beginning of a new direction for me.

Our oldest son, Errol, returned to Fresno shortly afterward and was hired at St. Agnes as a pharmacy technician. The rest of the family stayed in Flint until Janet completed her high school senior year. Before the family returned to California, I wanted to purchase a house in the Northwest Fresno community because of the high quality of the schools there.

I located a nice three-bedroom house in the desirable Fig Garden area, but the neighbors didn't want an African American in the community and the owner wouldn't sell to us. Even in the liberal state of California, housing dis- crimination was alive and well. In my view, it was a way some white people tried to maintain segregation.

I continued my search and found another three-bedroom house in a different section of Northwest Fresno; it was owned by an employee of a well-known financial institution. The employee was transferred out of the area and his employer, who had purchased the house, was willing to sell to us. We purchased the house in 1979 and lived there for ten years. The house had a nice backyard and a pool. We added a screened patio and expanded the master bedroom, which made the house more comfortable. We wanted our youngest son, Nelson Joseph, to complete his high school education at Bullard High School; he would graduate from Bullard in 1980.

Peggy, Janet, and Nelson Joseph made the trip from Flint to their new home in Fresno by car in mid-January 1979 and experienced winter storms along the way. The weather was cold and the highways, very slick. The severe traffic conditions especially in the state of Oklahoma were quite dangerous and challenging, and Peggy had to deal with black ice on the freeway. After the family got settled, Nelson Joseph got a part-time job at St. Agnes in the supply and materials department and Janet was hired as full-time employee at a nearby McDonald's restaurant. Peggy was successful in finding a position as an elementary school teacher at Bethune Elementary School in West Fresno.

TRANSFER TO THE PLANNING DEPARTMENT

Transferring to the planning department at St. Agnes was the beginning of a new direction, diversity in assignment, increased compensation, and career growth. I deeply appreciated the opportunity the CEO gave me and wanted to expand my knowledge and administrative skills. My responsibility as the junior planner was to help to develop St. Agnes Medical Center's long-range plan. I was challenged to quickly gain new knowledge and skills so that I could contribute to the planning department and the medical center.

Amazingly, the learning opportunity came sooner than expected., as the planning department was asked to develop a strategic plan for Mercy Hospital, a Catholic hospital in Merced, California. I worked with the senior planner, who had a bachelor's degree in planning. I conducted research, compiled data, and assisted in developing a strategic plan. We held meetings with the board of trustees and the Chief Executive Officer to review our findings and recommend a strategic direction for the hospital. After multiple meetings and plan revisions, the board accepted the five-year strategic plan for Mercy Hospital. As I continued to increase my knowledge and planning skills, and receive additional responsibility, I recognized the need for increasing my administrative knowledge and skills.

The ten years between 1979 and 1989 were the most rewarding times of my health care career; it was productive, I developed skills and I experienced professional growth. My title changed from assistant planning director (1982–1984) to director of research and planning (1984–1986) to director of corporate relations (1984–1986). My most significant contributions included designing and creating a territorial sales management system, which earned a copyright on September 19, 1988, and developing a corporate health risk management program. This program was created in collaboration with the vice-president of marketing and planning for the Palomar Pomerado Hospital District in Escondido and the coordinator of health promotion and wellness at St. Agnes Medical Center in Fresno. The program consisted of four steps:

- Identifying the health risk of the employee population
- Assessing the level of risk of each health factor for each employee, as well as the entire employee group
- Determining the financial impact of the rise
- Developing a risk-reduction strategy consisting of programs and inter- ventions to realize quantifiable net savings

The program was accepted and published in the March 1989 issue of the *Journal of Health Care Marketing*, volume 9, number 1, under the title "Corporate Health Risk Management: An Employer's Newest Tool to Reduce Health Care Costs."

In 1985, my supervisor, Ron Kelsey, the vice-president of marketing, resigned his position and accepted employment elsewhere, which resulted in a reorganization of the department. One of my peers, a female, was promoted to vice-president of marketing position and became my supervisor. We had previously worked together as peers, and I felt uncomfortable with the situation. Nevertheless, I continued to seek additional academic and employment growth opportunities.

My next goal was to pursue a master's degree in business administration. One of the major requirements for admission into an MBA program was taking the Graduate Record Examinations. Since I had previously taken the GRE when I began business courses at Pacific Lutheran University in Tacoma, Washington, I refused to retake the examination for admission to the School of Business at California State University. Unfortunately, my decision to challenge the gradu- ate school program advisor about retaking the test was a strategic error because the program advisor had the power to approve or reject applications. I was not admitted to the School of Business for graduate studies.

However, in October 1986, the dean of the School of Business and Administrative Services at California State honored me with a three-year appointment to the Business Advisory Council of the School of Business and Administrative Services. The advisory council included prominent business and civic leaders.

Despite the door closing on an MBA, I saw a new opportunity and decided to pursue a master's degree in public administration as there was some overlap in the two programs. It was another situation where I reset the pathway to overcome barriers and stumbling blocks to achieve my goal. As the Bible says, "Where there is a will, there is a way." I was later accepted to the MPA program at California State University, Long Beach, and earned a master's degree in public administration in 1982.

ST. JUDE INDUSTRIAL REHABILITATION CENTER

After working and living in Fresno for ten years, I was offered a unique opportunity in Southern California. The chief financial officer at St. Agnes Medical Center resigned his position and was hired as the Chief Financial Officer at St. Jude Medical Center in Fullerton. He surprised me by calling and inviting me to apply for a new administrative position in St. Jude's well-known and highly acclaimed rehabilitation department.

As a member of middle management at St. Agnes, I had infrequent contact with the CFO and was unaware that he'd observed the activities and management in my department. He arranged an interview for me with the vice-president of the rehabilitation department. In December 1989, I accepted a position as executive director of the industrial rehabilitation center, a new program that would be in Placentia, California, about ten miles from the medical center campus. I developed the business plan, created a vision, identified service components, and successfully opened the St. Jude Industrial Rehabilitation Center on October 29, 1990. I was highlighted, and the industrial rehabilitation center featured, in the January 7–13, 1991, issue of the *Orange County Business Journal.*

The rehabilitation center offered physical rehabilitation, counseling, pain clinics and job-training programs. The goal was to get injured employees back to work as quickly as possible. When an employee cannot return to their previ- ous job, they may be able to perform less strenuous tasks. The industrial rehabilitation staff included a physical therapist, occupational therapist, nurse, and psychologist, all working collaboratively with orthopedic physicians to deliver a holistic rehabilitation service.

Peggy remained in Fresno where she was employed as the principal of Baird Elementary School. We maintained a commuter marriage for one year. On Friday afternoon, Peggy drove to Corona and returned to Fresno on Sunday afternoon. I rented a one-bedroom apartment in Anaheim, California, about eight miles from my workplace in Placentia. On weekends, Peggy and I began to look for a house within twenty minutes of my work. We searched for an affordable house in Fullerton, Diamond Bar and Corona.

There was a housing boom in Corona, where we found the most affordable prices. We purchased a new four-bedroom house about eighteen miles from my work. The mortgage lender stipulated that Peggy must remain employed in Fresno until she secured employment in Southern California. We moved into our new home on Juniper Drive, and Peggy continued to commute by air for interviews and by car for weekend stays. She interviewed with school districts in Santa Ana, Orange, Compton, Beaumont, Hemet, Tustin, Riverside and San Bernardino. Many of the districts in which she interviewed would not hire an African American. She was finally offered a position as vice-principal with the San Bernardino Unified School District and was later promoted to principal where she worked for twelve years.

In 1990, the executive who invited me to St. Jude accepted a similar position at Little Company of Mary Hospital in Torrance. Shortly after his departure, my world began to crumble. At that time, I was the only African American middle manager on staff. The vice-president of the rehabilitation department then relieved me of my position at the industrial rehabilitation center.

Fortunately, I had a great relationship with my staff; they came out strong in support of me and protested my removal. Nevertheless, I was reassigned as the director of senior services and would be reporting to a female vice-president. The reassignment was punitive and laced with pitfalls and rabbit holes designed for me to fail and be fired. My first task as the new Director of Senior Services was to terminate the current director, a nurse who had held the position for three years, because the vice-president was dissatisfied with her performance. This nurse had completed a successful nursing career at St. Jude and, when she could no longer perform floor nursing, she was reassigned to an administrative position. This nurse was well known throughout the medical center and had a host of supporters, and she was white. It would have been suicide for me to proceed with that termination. Therefore, I took no punitive actions against her; instead, I decided to use the opportunity to learn from her.

Despite my limited knowledge of the position requirements and performance expectations, I was determined to do my best. I enrolled in and completed a one-year study in a gerontology program at California State University and earned a certificate in gerontology in 1992. Unfortunately, acquiring new knowledge and skills to enhance my credibility and performance made little difference with my female vice-president. She was a micromanager and required me to obtain her approval before doing anything or taking any action in the senior services department. As our relationship continued to deteriorate, it became apparent that it was time for me to seek employment elsewhere.

ST. FRANCIS MEDICAL CENTER

Fortunately, my blessing came just in time; God always provides a way for those who believe and are faithful. In 1992, the former CFO at St. Jude accepted a position as chief operating officer at St. Francis Medical Center, Lynwood, and invited me to apply for a key position at the center and arranged an interview with the vice-president of professional services. I accepted a position at St. Francis as director of sales with the focus on marketing a work-injury program to companies in Southeast Los Angeles communities. Later, the medical center affiliated with a health maintenance organization in Long Beach that served Medicaid clients. After they entered into an agreement to increase enrolment, I expanded my skills through marketing and sales of health care insurance for Medicaid patients, outpatient clinic development and management. I established a sales force to market health care insurance to prospective clients at community events, swap meets, street fairs and public celebrations to encourage enrolment. The sales efforts were extremely successful and brought new patients to the medical center.

As I continued to refine my skills and accepted new professional challenges, I was assigned additional responsibilities and new positions including director of occupational health services, and director of marketing and sales. As the marketing and sales director, I worked closely with the chief engineer to acquire property locations in Southeast Los Angeles communities and open ambulatory clinics. Once a suitable site had been selected and building improvements completed, I secured the appropriate license, purchased equipment, hired, and trained staff, executed the marketing plan for each location, and coordinated the blessing and opening ceremony.

After the clinics were established, I was selected to be the manager and promoted to Director of Ambulatory Clinics. I managed eleven primary care clinics in Southeast Los Angeles communities, including Compton, Downey, Huntington Park, Long Beach, Lynwood, Maywood, Paramount, and South Gate. Each clinic was staffed with four to five associates, mostly female. Oversight was provided by a contracting medical director who employed nurse practitioners to provide medical care. The clinic's scope of services included immunizations, prenatal care, and basic ambulatory care to the low socioeconomic populations in Southwest Los Angeles communities., and served as a feeder for inpatient care at St. Francis Medical Center, Lynwood, CA. The five clinics that remained operational in 2002 included Compton, Downey, Huntington Park, Lynwood, and South Gate. In June 2002, I retired from St. Francis Medical Center.

For many years, when Lynwood was a predominantly white community, St. Francis Medical Center only served white patients. Over several decades, St. Francis developed into a major health care institution that serves all patients who need care; it also offers open heart surgery, cancer treatment, short-term nursing care, obstetrics, orthopedics, and twenty-four-hour level-one emergency care. IN addition, the physical plant was upgraded, and the infrastructure rebuilt. At the time I worked there, St. Francis was owned and operated by the Daughters of Charity.

It is interesting that, throughout my successful innovative and productive career in health care, I was never offered a position at the executive management level. The highest title I held was executive director. Wit expansion of my knowledge and skills, promotions, increased responsibility and compensation, my new titles were always as "director" which kept me in middle management. I often believe that the privileged class is uncomfortable with an African American in the board room.

FOWLKES DEVELOPMENT GROUP

In 1992, I established the Fowlkes Development Group, a private health care consulting business. The purpose of the business was to assist health care organizations plan for such program expansions as industrial health clinics and worker's rehabilitation programs. My first client was an integrated health care delivery system. This organization brought together physicians and health care services of St. Agnes Medical Center and its affiliated entities to provide high quality coordinated heath care at reasonable rates. In 1994, I developed an organizational and market feasibility study for the public health service to determine the market demand for an occupational medicine program.

The nursing division at California State University in Dominguez Hills, California, was my second client. In 1995, I coordinated the Elizabeth Street Health Center Program implementation at Elizabeth Street Learning Center located in Cudahy, California. The Elizabeth Street center is a Kellogg-funded collaborative school-based project with California State University, Los Angeles School District and St. Francis Medical Center. As the project coordinator, I supervised all aspects of implementing the program including procur- ing equipment and supplies; hiring and training clerical, technical and support staff; securing a Cudahy business license; supervising the creation or revision of policies and procedures; arranging for housekeeping services; coordinating the installation of all operating systems—telephone, fax, modems, computers, printers, patient registration software, copy machine, transportation, supplies, specimen pick-up, mail delivery, interoffice mail distribution and waste dis- posal—and coordinating the department of health services facility inspection and licensing process. The center opened on July17, 1995, and received its health services license on August 5, 1995.

CHAPTER 11
Educational Benefits

The pursuit of education as a strategy has resulted in an enjoyable, rewarding, and comfortable lifestyle. I have benefited both personally and professionally from the knowledge and skills I've acquired through education. Looking back at my educational pursuits and their benefits reminds me that "I can do all things through Christ who strengthens me."

My educational journey began in 1953 when I was admitted to Central State University and successfully graduated four years later with honors. Then the blessing from the Department of the Army afforded me the opportunity to study biochemistry at the University of Tennessee, Memphis Campus, where I victoriously attained a master's degree in biochemistry. As a science major, I recognized my weakness in administration and management and the solution to this was a master's degree in public administration, in 1982, from the California State University, Long Beach. The combination of science and management gave me a good balance for future growth.

Between 1984 and 1988, I was involved in a variety of projects and diverse assignments and recognized for my achievements. In 1984, I received an appointment as an adjunct faculty member of the University of San Francisco, College of Professional Studies for the academic year.

In 1985, I was invited to serve as member of faculty in the department of health science at California State University, Fresno, for the fall semester, teaching a strategic planning and health marketing course. I also held faculty positions at Golden Gate, where I taught health care marketing to adult working students who lived in Merced, California, and were seeking to improve their knowledge of and skills in community health systems.

In 1986, I taught a three-unit marketing health services course. I taught other courses in health leadership and alternative community health systems. That same year, the dean of the School of Business and Administrative Services honored me with a three-year appointment to the Business Advisory Life Partner Council, which consisted of prominent business and civic leaders.

In 1988, I had the unique opportunity to collaborate with a vice-president of marketing and a nurse at St. Agnes Hospital to co-author an article published in the March 1989 issue of *Journal of Health Care Marketing*. That same year, I also designed and created the Territorial Sales Management System, which was my most significant development and achievement. This system is an innovative approach that applies traditional risk management to the health of an employee group. My system was issued a copyright on September 19, 1988, by the United States Copyright Office, Library of Congress.

In 1992, I established the Fowlkes Development Corporation, a private health care consulting business that assists health care organizations plan for industrial health clinics and worker's rehabilitation programs.

In 2005, I was appointed to the visiting committee for the Bureau for Private Postsecondary and Vocational Education. The bureau is the regulatory agency for postsecondary institutions in California. As a committee member, I conducted qualitative site reviews of applications.

By always seeking to better myself and gain more knowledge, so many opportunities for personal growth have come my way.

CHAPTER 12
Spiritual Development

My spiritual foundation and Christian values began with my surrogate parents, Reverend R.G. Gardner, and Cousin Odessa Gardner and continued when I returned to live with my biological family in Chattanooga. My mother was instrumental in expanding my spiritual growth by taking me to Sunday school and worship service at the Second Baptist Church, a short walk from our house on Grove Place. When the family moved to Blackford Street in East Chattanooga, I worshipped at the Prospect Baptist Church. After I moved to Cleveland, Uncle Charles and Aunt Amanda provided guidance and encouragement. Additionally, I was influenced by my grandparents, uncles and aunts, close adult cousins and schoolteachers. In Cleveland, I worshipped at the Liberty Hill Baptist Church on Kinsman Road. My situation presents a good example of the village having a major impact on my spiritual growth and devel- opment through guidance, support, and encouragement.

While a graduate student at Iowa State, one Sunday, I attended worship service at a church near the campus where the congregants were predominantly white. When I entered the church and sat on a pew in the center section of the church, all the white worshippers moved, leaving me as the only person on the pew. I was stunned. I felt embarrassed, hurt, and humiliated, and I was afraid to leave. Since I didn't know what to do, I stayed there. The minister observed the situation and made eye contact with me. I could tell he was concerned about what had happened.

As I sat there, I wondered how this type of treatment could occur in a house of worship where love should abound, not evil. God directs us to first love the Lord and second love our neighbors as ourselves. Immediately after the close of service, the minister came up and apologized for the display of racism. He gave me assurance that on subsequent visits there would be no recurrence of that behavior.

Peggy obtained her spiritual development and Christian experiences through the African Methodist Episcopal Church (also known as AME Church). Peggy was an active member of St. Paul AME Church in Lexington throughout her youth and teenage years. After starting a family, I wanted the family to worship together. Therefore, I changed my denomination to the African Methodist Episcopal Church. We faithfully attended bible study and services wherever we lived.

While on active military service, my wife and I actively participated in worship service at military installations or nearby communities. In Japan, we served as choir members at the military chapel in Camp Zama. In San Francisco, the family established membership at Bethel AME Church where we were active choir members. While living in Memphis, my wife and I served as choir members at Avery Chapel AME Church, and the children participated in the children's ministry. After a two-year graduate study in Memphis, my next assignment took me to Tacoma, Washington. From 1970- to 1975, our family affiliated with First AME Church in Seattle, sixty-five from our residence in Tacoma, Nevertheless, my wife and I made a commitment to attend on a regular basis and joined one of the choirs.

After my release from active military service, we moved to Flint, Michigan, and affiliated with the Vernon Chapel AME Church, where Peggy and I served as choir members. Later, when the family returned to California and lived in Fresno for ten years, we became active members of the Carter Memorial AME Church. During our time in Fresno, I served on the board of trustees and Peggy served on the steward board. We both sang in the choir and our children were active in the youth programs and activities.

In December 1989, my wife and I moved to Corona; however, our children remained in Northern California—Errol and Nelson Joseph in Fresno and Janet in Palo Alto. There were three AME Churches in Southern California within a thirty-minute drive from our house, located in Riverside, San Bernardino, and Santa Ana. We chose the church in Santa Ana, the Johnson AME Chapel, because we already knew about the church from the former pastor. While members at Johnson Chapel, we served as choir members. Peggy was also active with the Women's Missionary Society. I served as trustee for one year and steward vice-chair under pastoral administrations from 1992 until 2013. We were members of Johnson Chapel for twenty-three years, from 1990 to 2013.

In November 2013, we moved to Northern California and lived in Dublin. We now live in San Ramon, California. We were encouraged by our former pastor at Johnson Chapel to cast our membership with Brookins AME Church in

East Oakland, which is twenty-five miles from San Ramon. We joined the Brookins family in 2014. Our former pastor's family are members at Brookins, and they gladly welcomed us as family.

We are grateful and have been tremendously blessed by our former pastor's family.

CHAPTER 13
Adventurous Lifestyle

Living in different places for short periods of time and traveling frequently is a distinguishing characteristic of military life. My assignments were necessary to meet military needs or receive military or civilian training. The average length of each assignment was three years, except for school training and service in Vietnam. During my military career, I had the opportunity to live in and visit international and domestic locations including Japan (four years); Vietnam (one year); South Korea (one month); San Antonio, Texas (two years); Lawton, Oklahoma (three years); San Rafael and San Francisco, California (two years); Memphis, Tennessee (two years); and Tacoma, Washington (four years).

The army emphasized that the active-duty member was responsible for teaching and guiding their children how to be good citizens, respect authority and obey laws. Failure to do so could be reflected in the military member's evaluation. Living on the military installation was safe and somewhat protected from most events and activities occurring in the civilian world.

The military installation was like a city. It offered a wide range of services and recreational activities including schools; movie theaters; fitness centers; golf courses; athletic fields for football, baseball, and soccer; post exchanges (small department stores); commissary (supermarket); and fast-food restaurants. Military life also provided an opportunity to travel.

The military lifestyle was expensive because of frequent moves, the need to buy window coverings for each house, traveling long distances to visit family and the low pay during the early days of my career. I wanted the children to have a positive image of moving; my approach was to focus on the positive and fun aspects. At each new location, we became engaged in an interesting activity. Our lifestyle provided the family an opportunity to experience differ- ent cultures, develop new interests, acquire knowledge and skills, and engage in new activities.

In Oklahoma, the activity was outdoor living with cookouts and occasional visits to the Wichita Mountains Wildlife Refuge near Lawton. The refuge spanned over fifty-nine thousand acres. It was a place where several species of large mammals made their home, including the American Buffalo, elk, white-tailed deer, and Texas longhorn cattle. The children enjoyed the recreational activities at the refuge. Each year, West Point Cadets went for training at Fort Sill and were treated to buffalo steak before returning to the academy.

When we moved to Memphis, bowling became the family activity. Our children improved their bowling skills so much their peers wanted them on their teams. They gained a great deal of respect and admiration from their friends and participated in competitive team bowling events.

In Tacoma, the family took swimming lessons to gain confidence in the water and for enjoyment. We learned how to safely handle ourselves in water and passed the skill tests. The final test required the greatest level of confidence and courage. We were asked to dive or jump from the diving board into the deepest water in the pool come up and swim to the nearest wall.

During our first San Francisco assignment from 1966 to 1967, cycling was added to the children's bowling activities. Each Sunday, a portion of Golden Gate Park was closed off and reserved for children to ride tricycles or bicycles, or skate. Sundays at the park were fun and enjoyable. On my second San Francisco assignment in 1974, my living quarters on Infantry Terrace were directly across the street from two tennis courts. The entire family took tennis lessons and claimed the tennis courts as our private courts. We had a ping pong table in the basement of our house and held recreational and competitive ping pong games. We continued bowling, especially on Saturday afternoons, and I continued to pursue my cycling passion.

My adventurous lifestyle continued after being released from active military duty. In 1975, as my plane was landing in Fresno, I observed two things. First, cotton was growing on the land near the airport and, second, there was an abundance of swimming pools in the yards. Therefore, I wanted to purchase a home with a pool. We were blessed to make that dream become a reality.

The children enjoyed the pool and frequently invited their friends to the house for swimming parties. Many days, the temperature in Fresno exceeded one hundred degrees. I enjoyed swimming in the late evening and early morning before going to work. In Fresno, the family activities continued to be golf and swimming. Both Nelson Joseph and Errol became excellent golfers with scores consistently in the low-to-mid seventies. During a 2004 family reunion celebra- tion held in Philadelphia, Pennsylvania, Nelson Joseph played golf in the neigh- boring state of New Jersey and experienced the thrill of getting a hole-in-one.

In the '80s, roller skating became popular, and we quickly embraced it as a family activity. Errol, Janet, Nelson Joseph, and I purchased roller skates and frequently skated at the rinks in Fresno and Clovis. We worked diligently and with a great sense of purpose to develop unique individual and team skating skills with dance routines that we eagerly displayed. At the skating rink, the Fowlkes group attracted a lot of attention.

One summer, the family planned a skating weekend in Southern California. We started the trip from Fresno in two cars. Errol and his friend Mark rode in a Fiat convertible. I drove the second car, a small four-door sedan, with Peggy, Janet, and Nelson Joseph. While breezing through the Grapevine section of Interstate 5, the Fiat experienced a major malfunction near the Palmdale exit and had to be towed back to Fresno. This unexpected event required all six passengers and their luggage to continue the trip to Long Beach in the small over-crowded sedan.

When we arrived at the Holiday Inn in Long Beach where we had reservations, I rented a larger car that would comfortably accommodate six passengers. We checked into our rooms and had breakfast, then drove to Santa Monica. Our first skating event was a round trip from Santa Monica to Venice Beach. Next the fantastic Fowlkes skating group drove to an outdoor skating area in Newport Beach to skate and demonstrate our skills. We ended the wonderful weekend by skating at the well-known Flipper's Roller Rink in Los Angeles.

Even though the family enjoyed an active lifestyle, I experienced sorrow and pain when Peggy underwent open heart surgery in 2009 for an anatomical defect that prevented blood from getting to her lower limbs causing pain and limiting mobility. After dealing with the pain of walking and shortness of breath for two years, she agreed to corrective surgery. Peggy was blessed with a great thoracic surgeon who performed the surgery.

Shortly after the surgery, a nursing staff member advised the waiting family members, friends, and minister that we could visit with her within an hour. However, three hours later, no update or communication was given to us by the nursing staff. Later, we were informed that an unpleasant situation had occurred. At some point while Peggy was in intensive care, her heart stopped, and the medical team had to shock her heart to restart it. When we met with the surgeon, he explained to our family and friends what happened, that she was doing better and that he would stay with her throughout the night. I am convinced by this miracle that God loves his creation and has loved us from the beginning.

CHAPTER 14
Cycling My Passion

As a teenager in Chattanooga, I endured a major bicycle crash. Despite this, cycling became my passion. When I was a pharmacy delivery clerk, I had to ride a bicycle. While on active military duty, I continued to pursue my cycling passion, which became stronger after I moved to Fresno in 1978 and returned in 1979. I began riding in the neighborhood and later increased my distance by riding to Millerton Lake, a round trip of forty miles. As my cycling skills, endurance and stamina increased, I began participating in charity and fundrais- ing cycling events with distances of fifty to seventy-five miles. Even though the charity and fundraising cycling events required an entry fee or donation, the rides were enjoyable and well supported with rest stops equipped with restroom facilities, water, and food. Those rides were fun, adventurous, and challenging, with danger and safety concerns always present.

In 1988, while participating in a long seventy-five-mile fundraising ride in Fresno, I experienced a severe cycling crash. At times, I would get into a zone and may not be too observant of my surroundings. After riding for more than two hours in the bicycle lane on a rural highway, I was unaware that the bicycle lane had ended, and I was now riding on uneven jagged asphalt. As I was losing control of my bicycle, I did not attempt to apply my brakes, instead focused on falling away from the traffic flow. I had planned to land on the right side of my body; however, it didn't go exactly as planned. When I fell, my right shoulder took the major impact, fracturing my right clavicle. I remained on the ground for a little while, got up, brushed myself off and attempted to ride to the next rest stop less than a mile away. That's when I realized my shoulder was badly damaged. An emergency vehicle responded and transported me to St. Agnes

Medical Center where my two sons, Errol, and Nelson Joseph, worked. Later, I underwent surgery to repair the fractured clavicle, which involved inserting a metal screw into the bone to allow it to mend. Several weeks later, a second surgery was required to remove the stainless-steel screw. After rehabilitation, I returned to my cycling passion.

I continued to meet other cyclists and expanded my cycling diversity by participating in my first two-day century ride. A century ride is a bicycle ride of one hundred miles. One weekend, I was invited to go with a Fresno group to participate in a two-day ride to Santa Barbara. On arriving in Monterey, we mounted our bicycles and rode south to San Luis Obispo, where we spent the first night at a hotel. After breakfast on day two, we began the ride from San Luis Obispo to Santa Barbara. The last ten miles of the trip was on Highway 101 (south). With a tail wind at our back, this segment of the ride was exciting, thrilling and required minimum energy. We enjoyed a meal in Santa Barbara before being transported back to Fresno.

In Southern California, I continued to participate in well-supported fund-raising cycling events. My first event was a fifty-mile round trip ride from Corona to Lake Matthews sponsored by the Corona Lions. Before moving to Corona, I had invested in a high-quality Italian bicycle. The ride to Lake Matthews was challenging and involved a very steep and difficult hill to climb while sharing the road with cars and trucks. On the way down, several cyclists experienced accidents while traversing the treacherous and dangerous descending curves. As a result, the Lions stopped using that route for their annual fundraising event.

Shortly after moving to Corona, I became a member of the Riverside Bicycle Club, the oldest bicycle club west of the Mississippi. I continued recreational cycling and participated in club-sponsored rides as well solo rides from Corona to other California cities—Yorba Linda, Huntington Beach, Santa Ana, and Newport Beach.

Later, I desired to improve my power on the upstroke by getting a better foot-to-pedal connection. To improve pedal efficiency, cycling shoes and clip-less pedals are necessary. With clipless pedals, the rider is locked into the bicycle and must release one foot from the bicycle before stopping, otherwise the rider will fall. At a bicycle store in Fullerton, I talked with the owner, an avid cyclist, about purchasing cycling shoes and clipless pedals. The owner advised me to test the new clipless pedals by practicing falling in a grassy area. I felt insulted because of my diversified cycling experience.

However, I failed to realize that I had no previous training, experience, skills, or confidence in using clipless pedals. I was embarrassed on my first ride using them. I started the ride in the parking lot at California State University with members of a Los Angeles bicycle club called Different Spokes. Our route was a round trip from Fullerton to Irvine. Immediately after leaving the parking lot, I had to stop at a stoplight and fell because I was unable to get unclipped from the bicycle. During the ride, I experienced two additional falls. Fortunately, the seasoned riders understood my situation because they'd had similar experiences. Even though I wanted to just vanish out of sight, I had to endure the ride to the end and in the process learned a valuable riding lesson.

Between 1995 and 2007, I enthusiastically and vigorously pursued my cycling passion by participating in longer rides throughout Southern California. Following are highlights of my most enjoyable cycling tours:

TOUR DE PALM SPRINGS

The Tour de Palm Springs is an annual fundraising cycling event held on a Saturday during the month of March. The purpose of the event is to raise funds for multiple Palm Springs charities. The event attracts a wide range of beginner, recreational and avid cyclists from cities throughout Southern California. I participated in the event for five years.

On the Friday evening before the ride event, riders enjoy dinner and entertainment. I used my truck to transport my bicycle to Palm Springs on Friday afternoon and checked into the motel. It's important to make reservations at least three months in advance to get a motel room. On Saturday morning, after a continental breakfast at the motel, I rode my bicycle to the registration area to sign in and receive a route map. Music was provided by a high school band for the enjoyment of the cyclists, vendors, and spectators. Local police provided support along the major streets for traffic control.

Adult cyclists had a choice of four routes to choose from: one hundred miles, fifty miles, twenty-five miles and fifteen miles. The starter sent groups off by flights. The first group was one hundred miles at 7:00 a.m. The second group was fifty miles at 8:00 a.m. followed by the twenty-five-mile and fifteen-mile groups at 9:00 a.m. On my first Tour de Palm Spring cycling event, I chose the fifty-mile route but didn't realize there were challenging hills in the Palm Springs area. On subsequent years, I cycled with the twenty-five-mile group. My goal was to complete the ride in less than three hours so that I would have enough time to return to the motel, shower and check out at 12:00 p.m. I pursued a two-fold strategy to accomplish my goal. First, I did not stop at the first rest stop and, second, I maintained pace with the leading cyclists in my group. After checking out of the motel, I went to the Spa Casino in Palm Springs for a full-body massage.

CRUISIN' THE CONEJO

Cruisin' the Conejo was another favorite cycling event. For over thirty years, Cruisin' the Conejo has been the Conejo Valley's largest annual cycling charity event. The Conejo Valley spans parts of Ventura County and Los Angeles County that include the communities of Thousand Oaks, Westlake Village, Agoura Hills, and Calabasas. The event draws over a thousand riders, vendors, volunteers, and non-profit organizations from all over Southern California and the United States. It offers five routes that follow scenic backroads through orchards and vineyards, along the Pacific Ocean and through the beautiful Conejo Valley.

I got up early on ride day and drove sixty-five miles from Corona in Riverside County to Thousand Oaks in Ventura County. I participated in this ride for two years and chose the thirty-five-mile tour that started at 9:00 a.m. Cruisin' the Conejo is a difficult and challenging cycling event that reaches elevations of 1,786 feet.

TOUR DE SEWER

Tour de Sewer is an annual fundraising cycling event in Los Angeles County that draws over 1,000 cyclists; I participated in it for four years. The Bell Garden Lions has sponsored this event for thirty-five years. The tour starts at Ford Park in Bell Gardens and cyclists choose one of four routes ranging from a difficult sixty-two miles to an easy fifteen.

I chose the sixty-two-mile route the first year I participated. The route was challenging and went through the steep Whittier Hill with a fast switchback descent. The following years, I chose the forty-mile course; it had one moderate hill in Montebello and followed the Los Angeles and San Gabriel rivers, passing through the communities of Whittier, Montebello, Downey, Paramount, and Bell Gardens.

At the end of the ride, cyclists returned to the park to enjoy lunch and fellowship, listen to music, buy a raffle ticket for a chance to win a door prize and browse the colorful jerseys for sale. Over the years, I bought four colorful jerseys.

ONTARIO TO PALM SPRINGS

Ontario to Palm Springs is a two-day cycling event that I participated in for four years, further expanding my cycling experience. This event is s an annual fundraising event sponsored by a chapter of the National Multiple Sclerosis Society. Multiple sclerosis is an autoimmune disorder that attacks the central nervous system, brain, and spinal cord. There's no known cure but research continues to look for a cure and treatment programs provide temporary relief.

During the early years of my participation, cyclists were required to pay a registration fee and report $250 in contributions. Later, the contribution amount was raised to $400, which I could raise through donations or paying out of pocket. The ride started at Ontario Mills, a popular Southern California shopping outlet in Ontario, California. The route traveled through cities in San Bernardino and Riverside counties including Ontario, Rancho Cucamonga, Fontana, and San Bernardino, ending in Yucaipa Regional Park on day one. The last two miles are a tough, steady climb up the six percent grade to the park. At the end of day one, overnight accommodations are available at the park in the cyclists' personal tents or in a motel in Redlands. A shuttle bus is available to transport cyclists to their motels. I had a motel reservation in Redlands and took the shuttle. After a continental breakfast the next morning at the motel, I took the shuttle back to the park.

I started the day-two segment from the park with a thrilling downhill descent. The ride on the second day was moderate to easy but extremely excit- ing. We cycled through the communities of Calimesa and Cherry Valley, which run parallel to Interstate 10. The last segment of the ride is along Highway 111, the most direct route into Palm Springs. Usually, we encountered a tailwind that allowed for speeds of forty to fifty miles per hour with little effort. The ride ended at the senior center, where lunch was served. After lunch, I waited for Peggy to pick me up for the return trip home.

HUNTINGTON BEACH TO MISSION BAY

Huntington Beach to Mission Bay is a two-day annual fundraising ride that sup- ports a different chapter of the National Multiple Sclerosis Society, in Orange County. The entry fee is $200 plus $400 in donations or contributions. I took the opportunity to talk with several MS patients and this gave me a greater awareness of the struggles they faced and showed me how the money raised could positively impact their quality of life. The annual goal for the fundraising event is two to three million dollars.

I participated in the Bay-to-Bay ride for three years, from 2005 to 2007, and considered my support a labor of love and empathy for patients dealing with the affliction. San Diego cyclists are transported with their bicycles and luggage to Huntington Beach to begin the ride. All cyclists' luggage is transported to Carlsbad, California, for an overnight stay at the end of day one and then transported to Mission Bay where the ride ends. Cyclists from Orange, Riverside and Los Angeles counties are transported by bus to Huntington Beach while their bicycle and luggage are returned by truck.

On day one, the ride started at Huntington Beach, and we traveled through Newport Beach, Lake Forest, Mission Viejo, and Laguna Beach. At Monarch Beach, we followed the Coast Highway through Dana Point, passing by its picturesque harbor, and then into Doheny State Beach where lunch was served. We continued through San Clemente, passing the San Onofre power plant. The sponsors got permission for us to ride through Marine Corps Base Camp Pendleton and into Oceanside. (There was an alternative route along the section of Interstate 5 where bicycles are permitted.) After leaving the marine base, we returned to the coastline in Oceanside, where the road passed its harbor and pier. Upon arriving at the host hotel in the village of Carlsbad, we found food and entertainment waiting for us. I stored my bicycle in a secure area at the hotel parking lot and took the shuttle service to my motel.

On day two, the cyclists assembled at the host hotel for a continental breakfast and to check their bicycle tires for air and any needed adjustments. After breakfast, we continued along the route south, along the Coast Highway through the communities of Leucadia, Encinitas, Solana Beach and Del Mar. I began to experience pain in my legs while climbing the long and steep Torrey Pines Hill. At the top of the hill, the route passed the Torrey Pines Golf Course and the San Diego Campus of the University of California. Then dropped down into La Jolla (jewel by the sea) and turned inland at Pacific Beach toward the finish line at Hospitality Point in Mission Bay, San Diego.

At the end of the ride, lunch was served and accompanied by great music. Afterwards, I was transported by bus with other cyclists to Huntington Beach while our bicycle and luggage returned by truck.

NEW HAMPSHIRE MULTIPLE-DAY TOUR

I continued to expand my cycling horizon and decided to participate in a multi-day cycling tour. My first experience was in the New England state of New Hampshire during the foliage change. Bike Vermont, Inc. was a bicycling-touring company offering a three-day tour that began at Moose Mountain Lodge in Etna, New Hampshire. I took a flight from Los Angeles to Manchester, New Hampshire, and rented a car to drive to Etna. On September 12, 2000, I arrived at the Moose Mountain Lodge, a bed and breakfast that was a rustic log-

and-stone lodge perched on a secluded mountaintop. The complete package included accommodations, meals, and a bike tour. Owners at the lodge were friendly, and breakfast and dinner meals were excellent. Lunch was either prepared by the tour guides or we ate at local restaurants.

There was no telephone or television at the lodge. I met and rode with many interesting people who enjoyed cycling in different parts of the world. The group was made up of couples and singles; I was by myself and the only African American.

My accommodations were great. Each morning, our guide took a different route that included a full range of easy terrain mixed with moderate hills. I was blessed and rewarded to see God's handiwork in the red, brown, and orange leaves, which i seldom saw in California. The guide provided information on the history and cultural differences in the communities we traveled through as we crossed over the Connecticut River into Vermont, hanging out for a while at Dartmouth College in Hanover. One seventy-two-year-old man in the group shared a tremendous success story with us; he'd trained for six months and had participated in a ride across America.

CALIFORNIA WINE COUNTRY TOUR

My second multi-day cycling tour was offered by the Napa Valley Touring Company. The cost was $1,800 per person with nightly accommodation at a luxury bed and breakfast. My wife and I drove from Corona to Sonoma County to join the tour. Peggy was a faithful supporter who rode in the support vehicle. On day one, the ride started at Yountville Park and continued along manicured vineyards and old farmhouses, stopping at the Etude Winery for lunch and a private wine tasting. At the end of day one, we experienced the luxury of the Fairmont Sonoma Mission Inn and Spa.

The next day after a leisurely breakfast, the route took the cyclists toward Matanzas Creek Winery, and we passed through such charming towns as Graton (now home to a Native American casino) and Occidental. At the end of day two, we stayed at Bodega Bay Lodge along the ocean. On day three, the group cycled toward Healdsburg, and we spent the night at Madrona Manor. On day four, we cycled on a rolling route that led us to Alexander and Knights valleys. After wine tasting and enjoying a picnic lunch, I hopped into the van with Peggy for a lift to Calistoga Lodge where we spent the night.

Day five began with a climb into the foothills of Napa Valley and lunch at Velo Vino, which was known for delicious wine. We enjoyed dinner at

Michelin and lodgings at Lodge Solage. On the last day, cyclists had an option of taking a sixteen-mile cycling loop or relaxing at the lodge, indulging in a spa treatment or massage. I chose the sixteen-mile loop. After gathering for lunch, the tour ended, and cyclists were driven to the parking lot where our cars were parked. After a wonderful, awesome week, we drove back home to Corona.

AMTRAK CENTURY BIKE RIDE

The Amtrak Century is a scenic cycling event from Irvine to San Diego. The route is over flat to rolling terrain with an elevation of 3,200 feet. I participated in 1994. I began the ride at 6:30 a.m. from the Irvine Transportation Center. It had five rest stops and I had to arrive in San Diego at the train station before 3:00 p.m. to catch the train back to Irvine. This was my first attempt at riding one hundred miles in a single day. To prepare for my first century ride, I did several training rides from Corona to Newport Beach on the Santa Ana River Trail, a sixty-mile round trip with a maximum elevation of five hundred fifty-two feet.

My first century ride was a disaster, and I missed the train back to Irvine. My average speed was less than the fifteen miles per hour required to get me to San Diego by 3:00 p.m. First, I became comfortable at the lunch stop and lost track of time. Then, two unfortunate incidents occurred that contributed to my delay. While climbing the Torrey Pines Hill, I lost my route map. Then at the top of the hill, I got a flat tire. After changing tubes and inflating the tire, I was unsure of the route to the train station.

At a major three-way intersection, I had two choices, either right or left. I chose right, which was the wrong direction to downtown San Diego and the train station; I went ten miles in the opposite direction. My wife and daughter had planned to spend the weekend with me in San Diego and they went to the train station to meet my train. After a long delay they became concerned, but I finally reached the train station at 6:00 p.m. We enjoyed the weekend in San Diego, but I didn't attempt another century ride.

CHAPTER 15
Leisure Travel Business

As a young girl, Peggy held a deep yearning for travel. One of her most important childhood dreams was to work in the airline industry as a reservation clerk at an airport. As a youth and teenager, she traveled with her church for school activities and as a member of a singing group. At Central State University, Peggy was honored by the music professor as the first non-music major to get to sing with the Traveling College Ensemble. In September 2007, she fulfilled, in part, her childhood dream of working in the airline industry by opening a travel agency.

Peggy along with another interested person at Johnson Chapel AME Church in Santa Ana attended a presentation on how to become a travel agent. The idea took traction with Peggy, and she started a business called PJ's Travel Connection, a home-based travel business with a $10,000 line of credit from our local bank.

Peggy quickly learned that most home-based travel businesses are affiliated with a host agency for training, technical support, access to preferred suppliers, marketplace credentials and search engine availability. She first affiliated with Global Travel International based in Maitland, Florida. Because GTI didn't provide adequate training or support, or demonstrate an interest in growing her business, she began to look for a host agency that provided a broad range of services including web presence, training, support, marketplace credentials, high credibility in the travel industry, search engine availability and access to preferred suppliers.

In March 2008, while attending the annual Home-Based Expo and Luxury Travel Show in Las Vegas, Peggy met the president of Montrose Travel Agency's home-based division and became affiliated as an independent contractor. Through the affiliation, Montrose provided an interactive website with search engine capability, training (annual meetings and webinars), guidance and support. I was appointed by Peggy to serve as PJ's Travel Connection's business manager with responsibility for marketing and sales.

The beginning of my passion for travel had be enignited by military assignments, which required me to go by ship, airplane, and automobile from one destination to another. During my military career, I traveled many times from the west coast to the east coast and back again to visit family and friends. Once I became a co-owner of PJ's Travel Connection, my passion for selling travel to clients increased as well, which increased the opportunities for business and personal travel. As the marketing and sales manager, I was the interface between prospective customers and network groups. I was also responsible for the marketing materials—flyers and social media. My goal was to help our clients' travel dreams become a reality.

We gained product knowledge by attending annual trade shows and educational conferences, making hotel and resort site visits, doing ship inspections, and listening to webinars. We continued to expand our expertise as professional travel consultants through the acquisition of industry credentials and certifications including as accredited cruise counsellors. The cruise counsellor certification is one of the premier certifications for travel agents, especially those who market services to prospective cruise clients. Other credentials that we obtained included the Princess Cruises Commodore certification and the Carnival and Norwegian specialist credentials. We also established membership with professional travel organizations within the industry, including the Cruise Lines International Association, the American Society of Travel Agents, and the National Association of Career Travel Agents.

Military travel, both personal and business, provided me the opportunity to visit four continents (Africa, Asia, Europe, and North America). I visited Tunis in North Africa and destinations in Asia including Japan, Okinawa Island, Taiwan, South Korea, and Vietnam. Our European trips included Italy, France, Spain, Denmark, Monte Carlo, and Switzerland. In North America, we traveled to Alaska, Canada, Hawaii, and Mexico, and crossed the Unites States several times. I also had the privilege of visiting many Caribbean destinations including Antigua, Barbuda, Aruba, Barbados, Bahamas, Bermuda, Grand Cayman Islands, Puerto Rico, St. Lucia, St. Maarten, Puerto Rico and the U.S. Virgin Islands—St. Thomas, St. Kitts, and St. Croix.

My transatlantic crossing in April 2016 was my longest trip (seventeen days) and my most memorable cruise. It was a major contrast to the transpacific cruise I took in 1958 onboard a military transport ship. On April 29, 2016, my wife and I set sail in Fort Lauderdale, FL on the Royal Caribbean's Serenade of the Seas cruise ship. We reached land on day eight at Ponta Delgada in the Azores. We arrived in Cork, Ireland, on day eleven; Paris, France, on day thirteen; Bruges, Belgium, on day fourteen; Amsterdam, Netherlands, on day fifteen; and our destination in Copenhagen, Denmark, on day seventeen.

Here is a recap of the places I've visited:

European destinations	Belgium, Denmark, France, Iceland, Ireland, Netherlands, Switzerland, Turkey
North American destinations	Alaska, Hawaii, Mexico
Asian destinations	Japan, Okinawa, Vietnam

CHAPTER 16
Exploring Family Connections

During my teenage years, became interested in gaining information about my nuclear and extended family. These are some of the things I've learned.

My father, Eddie B. Fowlkes, married Dorothy Nelson, who was the first-born of General Nelson. They became the parents of four children, two girls and two boys: Edward Jr., Doris, Odessa, and little Nelson (me). Poverty and low socioeconomic circumstances prevented my parents and my siblings from pursuing a formal education. My mother was a smart woman, but she didn't have a formal education. We all had to get jobs at an early age.

During the war years, both my sisters married military men. Odessa married a young man who served in the Air Force, and they lived in Odessa, Texas. Doris married Charles Lowery, a young man in the coast guard, and they lived in Boston for a short time. Charles and Doris started their family, which included three children, Gary (now deceased), Sheila and Warbrit Russell. Unfortunately, for various reasons, neither marriage survived. Both sisters returned to Chattanooga and later remarried. Doris married Alfred Hamel and they had two children, Deborah, and Christine. Odessa married Tony Bradford (now deceased) and they had one daughter, Dianne. Odessa (now deceased), Alabama, and Doris lives in Douglasville, Georgia. My brother Edward is deceased.

Sheila, Doris's oldest daughter lived with us in Fort Lewis while attending nursing school, married Eugene Harvey and lives in Douglasville, Georgia. She had one son, Spencer, who is an active-duty military officer living in Texas. Deborah married Charles Robinson, a business executive, and lives in

Kennesaw, Georgia. Deborah's daughter, Demetri, married a minister and had one daugh- ter. Christine lives in Chattanooga.

Sally Sailes Fowlkes and William Thomas Fowlkes were my paternal grand-parents. I did not see or meet my grandfather; however, I frequently visited Grandmother Fowlkes, who lived in Chattanooga with Uncle Percy (her son) and Aunt Mary and spent a lot of time sitting in front of an open fireplace, my grandmother in her favorite rocking chair, and talking. I always wanted to stay long enough to be invited for lunch or dinner. Cousin Carrie Jefferson was another family member who lived close by—another favorite place to get a meal.

After moving to Cleveland to live with Uncle Charles and Aunt Amanda, I became aware that my father had five brothers including Booker T. (Columbus, Georgia), Charles (Cleveland, Ohio), Percy (Chattanooga), Thomas Jr. (the oldest son who lived in Maywood, Illinois, with his three children) and Robert Q. My father also had one sister, Edmona Fowlkes Penny. I was fortunate to have met Percy, Charles, Booker T., and Thomas Jr.

Frequently in the African American culture, the extended family is a source of financial support and serves as caregivers for older family members. When I moved to Cleveland, Uncle Charles and Aunt Amanda provided me a place to live, meals and guidance, while Uncle Booker gave me financial assistance at Central State University. Uncle Percy and Aunt Mary, who lived less than a block from our house on Grove Place, provided many meals and a warm house. As I reached out to find other relatives, I became aware of Uncle Thomas Jr. and his children.

My maternal grandmother, Della Elder, married Jake McDermott. "Nelson" is the root of my mother's family, which has two branches: "Roberson" and "Robinson." In 1977, my mother had a vision of starting a family celebration with the extended Nelson family and its branches. She also attempted to establish a joint family reunion celebration with the Elders (my grandmother's family) and the Nelson-Roberson-Robinson families (my mother's father's family members).

The joint family reunion with the Elders and the Nelson-Roberson-Robinson families started in 1978 and continued until 1982. In 1986, members from Nelson, Roberson and Robinson met in Birmingham and agreed to formally launch the Nelson-Roberson-Robinson family reunion. The first Nelson-Roberson-Robinson was held in Los Angeles in 1988, and the family members who attended decided to continue meeting bi-annually. Since meeting in Los Angeles, our families met in Fresno (1990); Atlanta, Georgia (1992, 2002, 2012); Waterbury, Connecticut (1999, 2010); Sacramento, California (1996, 2018) ; Cleveland, Ohio (1998, 2016); Chattanooga, Tennessee (2000); Philadelphia, Pennsylvania (2004); Houston, Texas (2006), Raleigh, North

Carolina (2008); and Torrance/Los Angeles, California (2014). The 2020 Family Reunion will be held in Dallas, TX.

Our family reunion has provided a vehicle forgetting to know one another better and the opportunity to pass on traditions, transmit values, enhance our individual and collective self-esteem, and appreciate the talents and skills within the family. At our family reunion, there is an outward expression of love and concern, demonstrated as family members embrace each other with joyful spirits. Love is also expressed in the way we speak and talk with each other, recognizing family member milestones such as birthdays and anniversaries.

After we married, Peggy and I became parents of two boys, Errol Allen and Nelson Joseph, and a daughter, Janet. Errol has two children, Merika and Errol II, and is now married to Babette. Merika and Error II in Las Vegas. Nelson Joseph has one son, Navan, from his first marriage. Navan is married to Melissa and has a son, Naecean and daughter, Veelah. Nelson Joseph is now married to Tracey, and they have two daughters, Halle, and Alexis. Halle is working for Amazon and Doordash in Fresno, and Alexia is a graduate form Baylor University in Waco, Texas. Janett has a daughter, Briana, graduated in May 2018 with honors from the University of Southern California in Los Angeles with a specialty in sound design.

Exploring family connections has been a rewarding and wonderful experience that has greatly enriched my life.

CHAPTER 17
Meaningful Retirement Life

God has blessed me and shown favor by giving me the opportunity to work and make contributions in three separate careers (military, health care marketing and health care management) and enjoy two retirements (from the military in 1978 and from St. Francis Medical Center in July 2002).

I planned my retirement agenda to include golf, cycling, traveling and relaxation. To improve my golfing skills, I had a three-hole putting green installed in the side yard of our house. Then I joined the Coupon Golfers, which consisted of retired truck drivers who played golf in the Riverside and San Bernardino County golf courses that offered discount coupons posted in local newspapers. Each golfer scanned the local newspapers and removed the golf coupons. At first, I liked the challenge and fellowship of playing competitive golf, but it didn't offer a lasting, fulfilling, productive or rewarding experience. After observing the golfer's language, practices, and character, I decided the most we had in common was playing golf. At the end of the golf round most of the guys ate lunch, told tall stories, and drank beer. My background, interests and lifestyle were vastly different from the retired truckers.

Consequently, I began to search for a retirement activity that was more challenging, stimulating and rewarding. I became aware of the Riverside Grand Jury. California is served by a jury system that provides a civil grand jury in each county empowered by law to bring indictments or perform an oversight func- tion into the operation of county government, municipal governments, and special districts. The work of the grand jury is done in committees. Each com- mittee is assigned a local governmental agency or department to investigate.

During the investigation, the grand jury acts as a finder of fact. The goal is to determine whether the governmental entity is operating in a businesslike manner and providing public services effectively and economically. The grand jury fact-finding efforts result in written reports, which contain specific problems and offer recommendations for improving government operations. The local government entity to which the report is directed is required to submit an answer to the county board of supervisors in writing within sixty to ninety days. An independent body determines which offices, departments and agencies will be investigated during its term of office.

The Riverside County Grand Jury is primarily a civil jury composed of nineteen members organized into five committees: administration and financial services, environmental and development services, health and community services, justice system, and city government and education. The duties of the civil grand jury are to act as the public's watchdog by investigating and reporting on the affairs of the local government, weigh allegations of misconduct against public officials and determine whether to present formal accusations requesting their removal from office, and review and act on letters of complaints from citizens of Riverside County.

In the spring of 2003, I applied to serve on the grand jury. My application was forwarded to the Grand Jury Recruitment/Selection Committee (judges of the superior court) to determine my qualifications for civil grand jury service investigation. I passed the Live Scan fingerprinting record check and was inter- viewed by judges of the superior court and a sitting member of the current grand jury. My name was placed for nomination by the interviewing judge.

My application continued through the process and was selected for drawing. Out of a pool of thirty nominated applicants, a random grand jury drawing and ceremony was held in June 2003. I was selected by the Presiding Judge, Riverside County Superior Court. as one of the nineteen persons to serve on the 2003–2004 Riverside Grand Jury. The remaining names from the pool of applicants were randomly drawn as alternates. At the end of the one-year term, the law permits up to ten outgoing grand jury members to be held over for continuity and training new members. At the end of my first year, I was selected to be held over to serve on the 2004–2005 grand jury. During my first and second grand jury terms, I served on the health and community service committee with three other members. This committee reviewed the Community Health Services Agency, Mental Health, Office on Aging and Riverside County Medical Center.

After sitting out for a year, I was nominated and selected to serve on the 2006–2007 grand jury panel. During that term, I served on the environmental and development services committee. The work of that committee focused on fire departments, waste management, the Economic Development Agency, date festival and fairs, information services, and purchasing and material. Again, I was selected to be held over for a second term and served on the 2007–2008 grand jury panel. I further expanded my grand jury experience by serving on the city government and education committee.

Even though I was nominated as an alternate for the 2009–2010 grand jury, I was not called to serve. However, I was nominated, selected, and served on the 2010–2011 grand jury. During this term, I served once again on the city government and education committee. One of the focuses of this committee was school districts, veteran services, city governments, the county office of education, charities, non-profit organizations, and libraries.

Once again, I was selected to serve on the 2011–2012 grand jury and was given the distinction and honor by the presiding judge of the superior court of being appointed foreperson for the 2011-2012 grand jury term. During my tenure as foreperson, administrative progress and improvements in the grand jury building were completed, including new furniture, and improved telephone and computer systems. The zenith of my service on the Riverside County Grand Jury was a feeling of civic duty and pride; not only did I learn more about the local and county governments, but I made recommendation for improving operations and service delivery to the citizens of Riverside County.

At the end of my grand jury service, I received training in conflict resolution with the goal of taking on small claims' cases. I enrolled in an online conflict resolution course followed by a three-day onsite training in Colorado Springs. When I completed the training, however, I was informed that, in Riverside County, only lawyers could be compensated for that type of work.

CHAPTER 18
Return to Northern California

I began my first California military assignment in 1967 at the Presidio of San Francisco and returned (1974-1976). I When I was employed at St. Agnes Medical Center (1979-1989) I lived in Fresno. After completing military service, I returned to California and lived in Fresno for ten years. In 1989, I moved to Southern California to work in Fullerton and later in Lynwood. We were empty nesters when we purchased the home in Corona. After I retired from St. Francis in 2002 and Peggy retired as a principal with San Bernardino Unified School District in 2003, we retained our residence in Corona and lived in Southern California for a total of twenty-four years.

Our children, however, remained in Northern California. Our daughter, Janet, lives in Palo Alto (a six-hour drive) and our sons, Errol, and Nelson Joseph, live in Fresno (a four-hour drive). The long driving distances were challenging for our children because of their work schedules and family responsibilities. Our access to our children and grandchildren was limited to Thanksgiving and Christmas, and some three-day weekends.

Several times, our children suggested we move back to Northern California. In 2013, Janet took the initiative and started looking for a desirable community in the East Bay area. We realized moving would require downsizing from a large two thousand three hundred square-foot house, so we held garage sales and donated items that we no longer needed. Janet began searching for apartments and townhouses in the East Bay communities of San Ramon and Dublin. so the mortgage balance was higher than the market value. Our home value declined from seven hundred thousand with a mortgage balance of five hundred twenty thousand to a market price of four hundred seventy-five thousand. This drastic decline placed us in a terrible financial position where we had to pay the mortgage, taxes, insurance, and maintenance on a property in which we no longer had any equity. Several times we applied for a loan modification. In one instance, we prepaid a company two thousand five hundred to assist us without any tangible benefit. Finally, we learned that our mortgage document, which was previously held by Fannie Mae, had been sold to a private mortgage company that was not interested in making any loan adjustments. Consequently, in June 2013, we entered a short sale contract to sell our home. The transaction did not close until April 2014.

In October 2013, my wife and daughter searched in the East Bay communities of San Ramon and Dublin for a suitable place. Several days later, I joined them in the search and selected a townhouse in Dublin. Now we are only forty-eight miles from Janet in Palo Alto, and a two-and-a-half-hour drive from Errol and Nelson Joseph in Fresno. Additionally, we live twenty-two miles from the Brookins AME Church in East Oakland where we worship.

CLOSING

Overcoming Adversity is a historical perspective of events that I experienced on my personal journey. These situations, circumstances, and events I encountered in life's pursuits required me to change and reset my goals, priorities, and strategies. Rejection and indignation were the two most painful and hurtful emotions I experienced because they attacked the very core, the very heart of me as a person created by God. Despite facing hardships and adversities, I was able to encourage myself.

I am reminded of the song "Sometimes You Have to Encourage Yourself." Despite life's tests, I continued to purse my educational goals and successfully managed three life-changing events: choosing a military career, being released from active military service, and starting a health care career. I did not allow my low socioeconomic beginning and dysfunctional family situation define me. I maintained a persistent attitude and employed different strategies to overcome the many obstacles, barriers and stumbling blocks I encountered in a segregated society where white Americans are privileged. I made mistakes, endured disappoints and dealt with despair while continuing to move forward with confidence, tenacity, faith, and trust in God.

In the decade of the '50s and before the passage of the *Civil Rights Act* of 1964, racism was blatant. After the act was passed, a brand-new form of racism emerged—one that was more subtle, yet just as insidious. I dealt with adversity and discrimination in accommodations, admission to institutions of higher learning, and perceived notions by some white people that African Americans were inferior and incapable of learning or performing at a higher level. I believe I destroyed that myth by my success earning a bachelor's degree in chemistry, two master's degrees in biochemistry and public administration, a professional certificate in gerontology and a certificate in conflict resolution.

Occasionally, there have been situations where a bright light was shining, for example, when a professor at the University of Tennessee Graduate School invited me to pursue a doctorate degree in biochemistry under his leadership. Another significant bright spot occurred when a chief financial officer became my champion. He invited me to apply for positions where he would be an executive and as he continued to move, I moved with him. Another touching and radiant occurrence was the encouragement I received from the white owner of a pharmacy in Chattanooga to get a college education.

My story reveals racism, discrimination and poor treatment experienced from individuals and institutions, at major universities and eating establishments, in places of worship and accommodations, and in military performance evaluations. Even though I had disappointments, setbacks and despair, the guiding principles in my life have been belief and trust in God, faith, hope and perseverance.

It is my hope that situations and circumstances illuminated in this story will help others to devise a successful strategy and pathway for dealing with opposition, barriers, stumbling blocks and disappointments they may encounter on their journey. According to the bible in into each life some rain will fall on the just and unjust. The difference is, for those who believe and have faith, God will give you the inner strength of the Holy Spirit to help you deal with and overcome issues.

DEDICATION

This book is dedicated to the readers who face barriers that adversely impact the attainment of their goals and dreams. However, through self-confidence, courage, self-reliance and using the most appropriate strategies and tactics you will be able to move forward and be successful...

ACKNOWLEDGMENTS

My story has been over five years unfolding. I am grateful for all the friends and family members who have encouraged and inspired me over the years.

I want to thank Peggy, my wife for her encouragement, understanding and help in recalling situations and events.

ABOUT THE AUTHOR

Nelson J Fowlkes is a retired Lt. Colonel who served twenty years in the United States Army Medical Service Corps. He earned master's degrees in Biochemistry and Public Administration. He also earned Professional Certificates in Gerontology and Conflict Resolution.

After retirement, he completed two careers in healthcare. As a strategic planning and marketing executive at St. Agnes Medical Center, Fresno, he co-authored the Five-Year Strategic Plan for a medical center in Merced. While serving as Director, Ambulatory Services at St. Francis Medical Center, Lynwood, he managed nine primary care clinics located in southeast Los Angeles Communities.

Fowlkes is co-author of a Corporate Health Risk Management Program published in the Journal of Healthcare Marketing. One of his most consequential achievements was the design and creation of a Territorial Management System (TSS), an innovative approach applying traditional risk management to the health of an employee group which the Library of Congress issued a Certificate of Recognition.

He was appointed adjunct professor at the University of San Francisco, College of Professional Studies in 1984 and at the California State University, Fresno in 1985. At both universities, he instructed adult working students who desired to improve their knowledge and skills in healthcare marketing and delivery of health care services.

His established the Fowlkes Development Group in 1992, a private consulting service company, to help health care organizations plan for the development and expansion of industrial health clinics and worker's rehabilitation programs. In 2004, the Presiding Judge, Riverside County Superior Court appointed him to serve on the Riverside County Civil Grand Jury 2004-2005 term. In California, a civil grand jury performs oversight functions for county govern- ment, inquires from the community on elected officials and other organiza- tions concerning any misconduct. He was reappointed to serve a total of three two-year terms (2004-2012) The Presiding Judge recognized hiss leadership on the grand jury with the appointment to serve as Foreperson for the 2011-2012 term.

Fowlkes expressed his adventurous spirit through cycling and traveling. In 1990, while living in Fresno, cycling became his passion. He acquired better equipment, improved cycling skills by participating in longer and more challenging fund-raising cycling events. After moving to southern California, he affiliated with a popular Riverside cycling club and expanded his cycling skills to include century and multi day rides. Expansion of the passion continued with cycling events in New Hampshire, Alaska, Jamaica, and St Maarten.

Cruising became a favorite pastime in 2007, when he and his wife started PJS Travel Connection, LLC, a travel agency that focused on serving clients who enjoyed cruising. Over a period of fourteen years, he visited cities in four continents, including Africa, Asia, Europe, North America and South America.

Today, he lives in Dublin,California.

www.ingramcontent.com/pod-product-compliance
Lightning Source LLC
Chambersburg PA
CBHW051223120626
46547CB00013B/1488